WriteTraits® TEACHER'S GUIDE

Vicki Spandel

Grade 8

Vicki Spandel

Vicki Spandel was codirector of the original teacher team that developed the six-trait model and has designed instructional materials for all grade levels. She has written several books, including *Creating Writers—Linking Writing Assessment and Instruction* (Longman), and is a former language arts teacher, journalist, technical writer, consultant, and scoring director for dozens of state, county, and district writing assessments.

Cover: Illustration by Claude Martinot Design

Design: The Mazer Corporation

Package and Cover Design: Great Source/Kristen Davis

Printed in the United States of America

International Standard Book Number: 0-669-49047-4

1 2 3 4 5 6 7 8 9 10 - MZ - 07 06 05 04 03 02

Contents

Introduction

Unit 1: Ideas

Unit 2: Organization

Unit 3: Voice

Unit 4: Word Choice

Unit 5: Sentence Fluency

Unit 6: Conventions

Welcome to the World of Traits!

With the *Write Traits® Classroom Kit,* we offer you a way of teaching writing that helps students understand what good writing is and how to achieve it. The kit provides instruction in six traits of effective writing. The term *trait,* as it is used here, refers to a characteristic or quality that defines writing. The six traits of writing, as defined by teachers themselves, are these:

- Ideas
- Organization
- Voice
- Word Choice
- Sentence Fluency
- Conventions

Six-trait writing is based on the premise that students who become strong self-assessors become better writers and revisers, and we are quite certain that you will find this to be true. No matter where your student writers are right now, we are sure you will see improvements in their skills. You will also see them gain the confidence that comes from knowing writer's language and having options for revision.

Components in the Write Traits® Classroom Kit

Each *Write Traits® Classroom Kit* contains the following components:

Teacher's Guide
The Teacher's Guide takes you step-by-step through each part of the program, from introducing the traits to presenting lessons to wrap-up activities that bring all traits together. Also contained in the Teacher's Guide are 6-point and 5-point reproducible rubrics and sample papers to practice scoring.

Student Traitbook
Available as a copymaster within the kit or for purchase for every student, the Student Traitbook contains all the practice exercises for the six traits.

Posters
Hang the two posters for students to use as a handy reference when revising their writing.

Self-stick Note Pads (package of 5)
Use these handy self-stick notes to indicate your scoring and comments so that you won't have to write directly on students' papers.

Overhead Transparencies
Use the transparencies for whole-class scoring or for discussion of the sample papers found in the back of the Teacher's Guide.

Writing Pockets
Available for purchase for every student, these writing pockets serve as a reminder to students of the six traits and as a place to store their writing in progress.

Teaching the Traits Units

The Teacher's Guide is organized into six units, one for each of the six traits. Each unit includes an overview, four lessons specifically designed to build strengths in that trait, and a unit wrap-up. At the end of the book are sample papers to use for practice in scoring papers.

Unit Overviews

Each of the six unit overviews accomplishes the following:

- defines the trait
- lists the instruction that will be emphasized
- provides a summary of each lesson
- contains two 6-point rubrics for scoring papers on the trait (one for the teacher, one for the student)
- recommends literature that can be used to model the trait

Traits Lessons

All twenty-four lessons, four for each of the six traits, follow the same format:

- Introduction, which includes an objective, skills focus, and suggested time frame
- Setting Up the Lesson, which introduces the main concepts of the lesson
- Teaching the Lesson, which provides teaching suggestions and answers for material in the Student Traitbook
- Extending the Lesson, which offers optional activities that carry the lesson concepts beyond the *Write Traits®* *Classroom Kit*

Unit Summaries

Each of the six unit summaries does the following:

- reviews the characteristics of the trait
- looks at the rubric
- applies the rubric to scoring sample papers

Warm-up and Wrap-up Activities

Warm-up activities are provided to help you introduce the concept of traits and the concept of analyzing writing by allowing students to assess right from the start. Warm-up activities help students think like writers and heighten their awareness of the traits within writing samples. The wrap-up activities are designed to show you whether students have a full grasp of the traits and can use all six of them together.

Using Rubrics To Score Papers

Rubrics and Checklists

Please note that a checklist is NOT a rubric. The checklist included on your kit poster simply offers students a convenient way of reviewing their writing to make sure that they have not forgotten any important elements of revision. The checklist includes no numbers and does not define performance at various levels along a rating scale. For this reason, neither you nor the students should use the checklist to assign scores.

Differences Between Rubrics

Our kit includes two 6-point rubrics for each trait, one for you and one for your students. We recognize that across the country, 4-, 5-, and 6-point scales are all in use. All have advantages. We believe, however, that the 6-point rubric reflects the greatest range of performance while still requiring raters to choose between generally strong papers (4s, 5s, or 6s) and papers in need of serious revision (1s, 2s, or 3s).

The 6-point rubric allows the assigning of an "above expectations" score of 6. Further, it divides the midpoint portion of the scoring range into two scores: 3 and 4. Think of a score of 3 on a 6-point rubric as a midrange performance, but one with a few more *weaknesses* than *strengths.* A score of 4, on the other hand, while also a midrange performance, has a few more *strengths* than *weaknesses.*

However, for your convenience we have also included 5-point rubrics, both teacher and student versions, in the appendix at the back of this Teacher's Guide.

Scoring Sample Papers

Sample papers included in this kit have been carefully selected to match precisely or very closely the grade level at which your students are writing. Some papers are informational; others are narrative. Some are well done; others reflect moderate to serious need for revision. These "in process" papers offer an excellent opportunity for students to practice revision skills on the work of others, and we recommend that you ask students to practice revising as many papers as time permits. This extended practice provides an excellent lead-in to the revision of their own work.

Suggested scores based on a 6-point rubric are provided for each paper. (Scores based on the 5-point rubric are in the appendix.) These scores are just that—*suggestions.* They reflect the thoughtful reading and assessment of trained teachers, but they should not be considered correct "answers." While no score is final, any score must be defensible, meaning that the scorer can defend it using the language of the rubric.

Frequently Asked Questions

How did this six-trait approach get started?

The *Write Traits® Classroom Kit* is based upon the six-trait model of writing instruction and assessment that teachers in the Beaverton, Oregon, School District developed in 1984. Because it has been so widely embraced by teachers at all grade levels, kindergarten through college, the model has since spread throughout the country—and much of the world. Traits themselves, of course, have been around as long as writing; writers have always needed intriguing ideas, good organization, a powerful voice, and so on. What is *new* is using consistent language with students to define writing at various levels of performance.

As a teacher, how can I make this program work for my students?

You can do several important things:

- Look to your students for answers; let them come up with their own ideas about what makes writing work, rather than simply giving them answers.
- Encourage students to be assessors and to verbalize their responses to many pieces of writing, including other students' work, professional writing, and your writing.
- Be a writer yourself, modeling steps within the writing process and encouraging students to use their increasing knowledge of the traits to coach you.
- Give students their own writing rubrics as you introduce each trait. Use the rubrics to assess writing and to help students see those rubrics as guides to revision.
- Share copies of rubrics with parents, too. This sharing encourages their involvement and helps them understand precisely how their children's writing is assessed.

Does six-trait instruction/assessment take the place of the writing process?

Absolutely not! The six-trait approach is meant to enhance and enrich a process-based approach to writing. Along with a wide set of options for revising, it gives students a language for talking and thinking like writers. Often students do not revise their writing thoroughly (or at all) because they have no idea what to do. Students who know the six traits have no difficulty thinking of ways to revise writing.

What do I do if I don't know a lot about the writing process?

Don't worry. We can help. First, you may wish to read the brief article by Jeff Hicks that summarizes the writing process. It appears on page xv of this Teacher's Guide and will give you all the basic information and terminology you need to work your way through the lessons without difficulty. If you would like to know more, refer to the Teacher Resources, page xviii. These resources will give you a strong background in the basics of the writing process, even if you've never been to a single workshop on the subject!

What do I have to give up from my current curriculum?

Nothing. If you are teaching writing through writers' workshops or any writing process–based approach, you will find that virtually everything you do is completely compatible with this program. It is ideally suited to process writing and particularly supports the steps of revision and editing.

Do I have to teach the traits in order?

We recommend that you teach both traits and lessons in the order presented because we use a sequential approach in which skills build on one another. Longer writing activities toward the end of each trait unit will require students to use the skills they have learned in studying a previous trait so that nothing is "lost." In other words, we do not want students to forget about *ideas* just because they move on to *organization.*

We do recognize, though, that most teachers prefer to teach conventions throughout the course of instruction, rather than as a separate unit. Therefore, incorporate instruction in conventions as you present the other traits.

Do all six traits ever come together?

Definitely. Writing should not be disjointed. We take it apart (into traits) to help students *master specific strategies for revision.* But eventually, we must put the slices of the pie back together. With this in mind, we provide several closure lessons, including one in which students will score a paper for all six traits and check their results with those of a partner. By this time, students will also be ready to assess and revise their own writing for all six traits. Wrap-up lessons may be assessed if you choose to do so.

Using Traits with the Writing Process

by Jeff Hicks

If writing were an act of fairy-tale magic or a matter of wishing, the word *process* would never apply to what people do when they write. All writers would have to do is wave their magic wands, rub their enchanted lamps to make their genies appear, or catch the one fish—from an ocean filled with fish—that grants wishes to the lucky person who hauls it in. *I'd like a bestseller about a pig and a spider who live on a farm. Allakazam! Presto! Newbery Medal!* Perhaps Roald Dahl was a fisherman and Beverly Cleary was a collector of antique lamps, right? Of course not! Writers understand that writing is a process involving multiple steps and plenty of time. An understanding of the process of writing is an important foundation for all young writers. Once they have the process in place, students can grasp and use the six traits of writing to help them revise and assess their own work. The six traits support the writing process.

The Writing Process The traditional view of the writing process is one that involves four or five steps or stages.

Prewriting
Drafting (Writing)
Revising
Editing
Publishing/Sharing

1. **Prewriting**—This is the stage in which the writer attempts to find a topic, narrow it, and map out a plan. The writer usually isn't concerned with creating whole sentences or paragraphs at this point. Prewriting is done *before* the writer begins to write, and it is aimed at defining an idea and getting it rolling.

2. **Drafting (Writing)**—In this stage, the writer's idea begins to come to life. Sentences and paragraphs begin to take shape. The writer may experiment with different leads. In this stage, writers need to know that they can change directions, cross out words or sentences, and draw arrows to link details that are out of sequence. The term *rough draft*, or *first draft,* refers to writers in motion, changing directions and letting their ideas take shape.

3. **Revising**—When writers revise, their topics and ideas come into focus. In this stage, writers do a great deal of math—adding or subtracting single words, phrases, or entire paragraphs. What to revise often becomes clearer to students if they have had some time away from their drafts. Putting a draft away, out of sight and mind, for a few days or even more, may provide a sharper focus on weak areas. A writer might even ask, "Did I really write this?" The efforts made at revision will easily separate strong writing from weak writing.

4. **Editing**—This stage is all about making a piece of writing more accessible to readers. In this stage, writers fine-tune their work by focusing on correct punctuation, capitalization, grammar, usage, and paragraphing. Writers will want to be open to all the technological help (spell checking, for example) and human help they can find.

5. **Publishing/Sharing**—Not every piece of writing reaches this stage. The term *sharing* refers here to something more public than the kind of interactive sharing that should be happening at the previous stages. When writing is going to be "published" in the classroom or put on display as finished work, it needs to have been carefully selected as a piece of writing that has truly experienced all the other stages of the writing process.

These steps are often presented in classrooms as being separate, mutually exclusive events. *If I'm prewriting, I can't be revising. If I'm drafting, I can't be editing. If I'm revising, I can't be editing.* Mature writers know that the process may proceed through the steps in linear fashion, one at a time, but it is more likely that the parts of the process will intertwine. The process doesn't seem so overwhelming if a young writer can gain this perspective. I like to teach students several prewriting strategies—webbing, outlining, making word caches, drawing, and developing a list of questions—but I also like to show them through my own writing that prewriting and drafting can occur simultaneously. Having students experience their teacher as a writer is the most powerful way to demonstrate the importance of each stage and how it connects with the others. For instance, the best way for me to prewrite is to begin "writing." It is the act of writing (drafting) that often gets my ideas flowing better than if I tried to make a web of the idea. Writing also allows me to demonstrate that I can revise at any time. I can cross out a sentence, change a word, draw an arrow to place a sentence in a different paragraph, add a few words, or move a whole paragraph; all of this can be done while I draft an idea. At the same time, I might even notice that I need to fix the spelling of a word or add a period—that's editing!

Bringing in the Traits I know that many young writers speak and act as if they have magical pens or pencils. In the classroom, these are the students who proclaim, "I'm done!" minutes after beginning, or they are the ones who say, "But I like it the way it is!" when faced with a teacher's suggestion to tell a bit more or to make a few changes. Other students frequently complain, "I don't have anything to write about." Immersing these students in the writing process with a teacher who is also a writer is the clearest path to silencing these comments. Throw into this mix a strong understanding of the six traits of writing, and you are well on your way to creating passionate, self-assessing writers.

Teacher Resources

The "Must-Have" List for Teaching Writing Using the Six Traits

Ballenger, Bruce. 1993. *The Curious Researcher: A Guide to Writing Research Papers.* Needham Heights, MA: Allyn & Bacon.

Blake, Gary and Robert W. Bly. 1993. *The Elements of Technical Writing.* New York: Macmillan.

Burdett, Lois. 1995. *Shakespeare Can Be Fun* (series). Willowdale, Ontario, and Buffalo, NY: Firefly Books.

Calkins, Lucy McCormick. 1994. *The Art of Teaching Writing.* 2nd. ed. Portsmouth, NH: Heinemann.

Claggett, Fran, et al. 1999. *Daybook of Critical Reading and Writing* (Grade 7). Wilmington, MA: Great Source.

Fletcher, Ralph and Joann Portalupi. 1998. *Craft Lessons: Teaching Writing K through 8.* Portland, ME: Stenhouse Publishers.

Fox, Mem. 1993. *Radical Reflections: Passionate Opinions on Teaching, Learning, and Living.* New York: Harcourt.

Frank, Marjorie. 1995. *If You're Trying to Teach Kids How to Write . . . you've gotta have this book!* 2nd. ed. Nashville: Incentive Publications, Inc.

Glynn, Carol. 2001. *Learning on Their Feet: A Sourcebook for Kinesthetic Learning Across the Curriculum K–8.* Shoreham, VT: Discover Writing Press.

Goldberg, Natalie. 1990. *Wild Mind.* New York: Bantam Books.

Graves, Donald H. 1986. *Writing: Teachers & Children at Work.* Portsmouth, NH: Heinemann.

Harvey, Stephanie. 1998. *Nonfiction Matters: Reading, Writing, and Research in Grades 3–8.* Portland, ME: Stenhouse Publishers.

Keene, Ellen Oliver, with Susan Zimmerman. *Mosaic of Thought: Teaching Comprehension in a Reader's Workshop.* 1997. Portsmouth, NH: Heinemann.

Kemper, Dave, et al. 1999. *Write Source 2000.* Wilmington, MA: Great Source.

Lamott, Anne. 1995. *Bird by Bird: Some Instructions on Writing and Life.* New York: Alfred A. Knopf.

Lane, Barry. 1993. *after THE END.* Portsmouth, NH: Heinemann.

Lane, Barry. 1998. *The Reviser's Toolbox.* Shoreham, VT: Discover Writing Press.

Lane, Barry, with Gretchen Bernabei. 2001. *Why We Must Run with Scissors: Voice Lessons in Persuasive Writing 3–12.* Shoreham, VT: Discover Writing Press.

Murray, Donald M. 1985. *A Writer Teaches Writing.* 2nd. ed. New York: Houghton Mifflin.

O'Conner, Patricia T. 1999. *Words Fail Me: What Everyone Who Writes Should Know About Writing.* New York: Harcourt.

Portalupi, Joann, with Ralph Fletcher. 2001. *Nonfiction Craft Lessons: Teaching Information Writing K–8.* Portland, ME: Stenhouse Publishers.

Romano, Tom. 1995. *Writing with Passion: Life Stories, Multiple Genres.* Portsmouth, NH: Boynton/Cook.

Spandel, Vicki. 2001. *Creating Writers.* 3rd. ed. New York: Allyn & Bacon.

Stiggins, Richard J. 1996. *Student-Centered Classroom Assessment.* 2nd. ed. Columbus, OH: Prentice Hall (Merrill).

Thomason, Tommy. 1998. *Writer to Writer: How to Conference Young Authors.* Norwood, MA: Christopher-Gordon Publishers.

Thomason, Tommy and Carol York: 2000. *Write on Target: Preparing Young Writers to Succeed on State Writing Achievement Tests.* Norwood, MA: Christopher-Gordon Publishers.

Zinsser, William. 2000. *On Writing Well: An Informal Guide to Writing Nonfiction.* 6th. ed. New York: HarperCollins.

Using Write Traits Classroom Kits with *Write Source 2000*

Write Traits Classroom Kit, Grade 8	Skill Focus	*Write Source 2000* © 1999
Unit 1: Ideas		
Lesson 1: Will It Fit in My Backpack?	Use prewriting strategies.	Prewriting: Choosing a Subject, pp. 45–52
Lesson 2: Setting the T-Table	Use sensory details in writing.	Using Gathering Strategies, pp. 54–58
Lesson 3: No Doubt About It	Include enough details.	Details in Paragraphs, p. 105
Lesson 4: Just Right	Omit filler.	Revising: Improving Your Writing, pp. 14–15
Unit 2: Organization		
Lesson 5: Looking for a Pattern	Be familiar with patterns of organization.	Methods of Organization, p. 60
Lesson 6: Finding the Perfect Match	Match the pattern to the purpose.	Revising for Organization, p. 71
Lesson 7: Clear Connections	Use transitions.	Transitions, p. 106
Lesson 8: Creating the Total Package	Organize a paragraph.	The Parts of a Paragraph, pp. 98–99
Unit 3: Voice		
Lesson 9: A Defining Moment	Define voice.	Engaging Voice, p. 22
Lesson 10: Keeping Readers Connected	Enhance voice with interest in the subject.	Writing Guidelines (Expository Essays), pp. 110–111
Lesson 11: Thinking About Audience	Match voice to the audience.	Five Keys to Good Revision, p. 69
Lesson 12: Kick It into High Gear!	Revise to enhance voice.	Revising for Voice, pp. 72–73

Unit 4: Word Choice		
Lesson 13: Right Word, Right Color, Right Picture	Use synonyms and antonyms.	Referring to a Thesaurus, p. 325
Lesson 14: Sensory Words	Use sensory language.	Original Word Choice, p. 22
Lesson 15: Call It As You See It	Use specific language.	Using Strong, Colorful Words, p. 135
Lesson 16: The Right Team for the Job	Cut out extra words.	Checking for Word Choice, p. 82
Unit 5: Sentence Fluency		
Lesson 17: My Shoes... My Shoes... My Shoes...	Vary sentence beginnings.	Smooth-Reading Sentences, p. 23
Lesson 18: Trucking in the Transitions	Use transitions judiciously.	Transitions, p. 106
Lesson 19: Famous for Flow	Analyze text for elements that contribute to fluency.	Checking for Sentence Smoothness, p. 81
Lesson 20: Smooth Sailing	Revise text for fluency.	Composing Sentences, pp. 85–92
Unit 6: Conventions		
Lesson 21: Straighten It Up	Distinguish between revising and editing.	One Writer's Process, pp. 9–18
Lesson 22: Gliding Down the Highway	Identify errors.	Editing and Proofreading, pp. 79–82
Lesson 23: How Symbolic!	Use editor's symbols.	Editing and Proofreading Marks, inside back cover
Lesson 24: The Editing Express Lane	Make an editing checklist.	Editing and Proofreading Checklist, p. 83

Write Traits® Classroom Kits SCOPE AND SEQUENCE

Trait/Skill	Grade 3	4	5	6	7	8
IDEAS						
Narrowing the Topic			•	•	•	•
Getting Started	•	•		•		•
Identifying the Main Idea	•	•	•			
Clarifying Ideas				•	•	•
Expanding Sketchy Writing			•	•	•	
Identifying What Is Important	•	•	•			
Making Writing Concise	•	•			•	•
ORGANIZATION						
Writing a Strong Lead	•	•	•			
Putting Things in Order	•		•		•	
Identifying Organizational Patterns		•		•		•
Matching Organizational Pattern and Writing Task		•		•		•
Staying on Topic	•		•		•	
Creating Strong Transitions				•	•	•
Writing Endings	•	•	•			
Putting Details Together				•	•	•
VOICE						
Defining Voice				•	•	•
Matching Voice and Purpose	•		•		•	
Putting Voice into Personal Narrative	•	•	•			
Putting Voice into Expository Writing				•	•	•
Matching Voice to Audience				•	•	•
Sharing Favorite Voices	•	•	•			
Putting Voice into Flat Writing		•		•		•
Using Personal Voice	•	•	•			

Trait/Skill	Grade 3	4	5	6	7	8
WORD CHOICE						
Using Strong Verbs	•	•	•			
Using Synonyms and Antonyms to Enhance Meaning				•	•	•
Inferring Meaning from Context	•	•	•			
Using Sensory Words to Create a Word Picture	•	•	•	•		•
Using Strong Words to Revise Flat Writing				•	•	•
Revising Overwritten Language		•		•	•	•
Eliminating Wordiness	•		•		•	
SENTENCE FLUENCY						
Making Choppy Writing Fluent	•		•		•	
Varying Sentence Beginnings	•	•				•
Varying Sentence Length			•	•	•	
Eliminating Run-ons	•	•		•		
Inserting Transitions				•	•	•
Creating Dialogue	•	•	•			
Assessing Fluency Through Interpretive Reading		•		•		•
Reading and Revising Personal Text			•		•	•
CONVENTIONS						
Distinguishing Between Revising and Editing		•	•	•	•	•
Spotting Errors	•		•		•	
Knowing the Symbols	•	•	•	•	•	•
Correcting Errors	•	•	•	•	•	•
Creating an Editing Checklist	•	•		•		•

Warm-up Activity 1 gives students an opportunity to read critically and see whether they can identify the main problem in a piece of writing. Students need not be familiar with the six traits to do this exercise. However, if students are new to the six traits, you may wish to introduce the activity by defining the word *trait* as a characteristic or quality that helps define an object or concept. Warm-up Activity 1 will take about 20 minutes. Warm-up Activity 2 asks students to review before-and-after samples to see whether they can recognize the kind of revision the writer has done. Again, students need not be familiar with the six traits to do this exercise. Warm-up Activity 2 will also take about 20 minutes.

Warm-up Activity 1

What's the Problem?

For use with Student Traitbook, pages 5–6

Students will not score these samples (so they do not need rubrics yet), but they will read each one carefully and mark the problem they think is most noticeable. They may notice more than one kind of problem, but in each case, one specific problem is obvious and clearly overrides any others. Students can work with partners on this warm-up activity. Discuss results with the entire class.

Sample 1 Rationale

Students should see that the main problem with this passage is **fluency.** Virtually every sentence begins the same way, and this monotonous characteristic should be obvious even if your students have not worked with traits previously and do not have a solid definition of the term fluency. The **organization** is sound: the writer does not wander from the main topic, nor is the paper hard to follow.

Sample 2 Rationale

Students should see that the main problem with this passage is **voice.** Although the writer provides good information, it is presented with almost no energy or enthusiasm. The writer sounds tired and bored. The **ideas** are fine. The piece *does* have a main idea: This is what to do to make a tasty cake. The writing is clear and provides sufficient information to get the message across.

Warm-up Activity 2

Name That Revision Strategy

For use with Student Traitbook, page 6

Students will not score this sample (so they do not need rubrics yet), but they will read it carefully and mark the best match to the kind of revision the writer has done. They may notice more than one kind of change, but the revision is highly focused, and it should be easy to pick out the changes the writer has made. Students can work with partners on this warm-up activity. Discuss results with the entire class.

Sample 1 Rationale

Again, there is more than one kind of change, but the standout revision is for **fluency.** The **word choice** is slightly different, but it's a minor change.

Extensions

1. Invite students to revise one of the samples from Warm-up Activity 1. They should focus on the trait they have identified as needing the most attention, but they may make other kinds of changes as well. Read results aloud, and discuss the changes students have made.

2. Brainstorm the key characteristics of each trait as your students envision them now. Ask them to keep these lists handy so that later, as you introduce each trait, they can compare their initial impressions with the Student Rubrics.

3. Ask students to identify the primary area they need to work on in their own writing. What are their strengths? They may wish to share their thoughts in small groups. Participate in this activity yourself, and share your thoughts with students.

4. Ask each student to list three things he or she has done recently (within the past year) to revise his or her writing. Make your own list as well. Then, ask students to work with partners to link each revision task with one of the six traits. Tell them that this is NOT a test. The idea is for them to begin linking the traits with actual revision. Share some examples, and let students know how you would link each revision strategy: adding information (ideas), deleting unneeded information (ideas), rewriting a lead or conclusion (organization), changing order (organization), changing the tone (voice), making the writing livelier (voice), changing the wording (word choice), putting in more verbs (word choice), beginning sentences differently (fluency), and so on.

5. Make some predictions or observations. Which trait do your students think they know most about right now? Which one will be most interesting? Most challenging? When they choose a book to read for fun, on which trait(s) do they most often base that choice?

WriteTraits®

TEACHER'S GUIDE

Overview

This unit focuses on the concept of ideas—the writer's primary message, point, or story. The lessons are all designed to help students clarify ideas, both in their minds and on paper. Students will analyze samples by professional writers, revise text for specific features, and create some writing of their own. In all cases, the emphasis will be on clarity, inclusion of important details, and elimination of wordy writing.

The focus of instruction in this unit will be

- making a big topic "fit" by narrowing the focus
- using a T-Table prewriting strategy
- transforming foggy writing into clear, detailed text
- eliminating the filler that confuses and distracts readers

Ideas: *A Definition*

Ideas are about information. Information can come from a writer's own experience, from research, from reading, or from talking with others. Knowing a topic well is the first step toward presenting strong ideas. In addition, the writer must select details that paint a clear picture in the reader's mind and eliminate filler—unnecessary information that clutters the writing. Three elements make ideas work well and should be the focus of your instruction: a *solid main idea* that's easy to identify and narrow enough to be manageable; *interesting details* that bring the main idea to life; and *clarity,* achieved in part through careful selection and presentation of details.

The Unit at a Glance

The following lessons in the Teacher's Guide and practice exercises in the Student Traitbook will help develop understanding of the trait of ideas. The Unit Summary provides an opportunity to practice evaluating papers for ideas.

Unit Introduction: Ideas

Teacher's Guide pages 2–6

The unique features of the trait of ideas are presented along with a rubric and a list of recommended books for teaching the trait of ideas.

Lesson 1: Will It Fit in My Backpack?

Teacher's Guide pages 7–9
Student Traitbook pages 7–11

In this lesson, students learn to make a topic "fit" within the scope of the writing by using probing questions that narrow a topic to a manageable size.

Lesson 2: Setting the T-Table

Teacher's Guide pages 10–12
Student Traitbook pages 12–15

As readers, students see pictures in their minds and also have reactions to the text. In this lesson, they learn one prewriting activity designed to heighten "seeing" and "feeling" details within their own writing.

Lesson 3: No Doubt About It

Teacher's Guide pages 13–15
Student Traitbook pages 16–19

Vague writing leaves readers with questions—or doubts. In this lesson, students learn to create writing that answers a reader's questions.

Lesson 4: Just Right

Teacher's Guide pages 16–18
Student Traitbook pages 20–23

Skimpy writing leaves readers with questions; overloaded writing piles on so many details that readers feel overwhelmed. In this lesson, students gain practice in spotting and eliminating filler to create clear text.

Unit Summary: Ideas

Teacher's Guide page 19
Overhead numbers 1–4

Use the student rubric on page 5 and the activities in the Summary to practice evaluating writing for the trait of ideas. Remember, 5-point rubrics, along with rationales for scores on sample papers, appear in the Appendix of this Teacher's Guide, pages 192–214.

Teacher Rubric for Ideas

6
- The paper is clear and focused. The topic is small and well defined.
- The message or story is both engaging and memorable.
- The writer seems to have in-depth understanding of the topic.
- The writer is selective, consistently sharing unusual, beyond-the-obvious details that are informative, entertaining, or both.

5
- This paper is mostly clear and focused. The topic is small enough to handle in the scope of the paper.
- The message/story has many engaging moments.
- The writer knows enough about the topic to do a thorough job.
- The writer has chosen many interesting or little-known details.

4
- The topic is fairly well defined, but it could be smaller.
- There are some engaging moments.
- The writer knows the topic reasonably well; more information would make this writing more interesting or helpful.
- The writing includes some interesting or unusual details. The writer needed to dig a little deeper, think harder, or do more research.

3
- It is fairly easy to guess what the main idea is. Some parts are unclear, however, or the topic is still too big to handle.
- There are few, if any, engaging moments.
- Sometimes the writer appears to know what he or she is talking about. At other times, the writer seems to struggle to fill the page.
- Detail is present, but some of it is too general.

2
- The main idea or story is still coming together. What is this writer trying to say?
- There are no engaging or memorable moments.
- The writer seems unsure about his or her message, and the main idea may be buried under too much information or not developed at all.
- Details are sketchy. The reader must guess the writer's meaning.

1
- This writer is still searching for a main idea—or story. It's not there yet.
- There are no engaging or memorable moments.
- The writing is too sketchy to have a main idea, or it consists of random thoughts or notes that share no apparent common theme.
- The reader cannot extract anything meaningful, even by guessing.

Student Rubric for Ideas

6
- My paper is crystal clear from the first sentence to the last. It is very easy to tell what my main idea is. I kept my topic small and focused.
- My message is very interesting and memorable.
- I know this topic very well.
- I was careful to choose many interesting, unusual details.

5
- I think this topic is well defined and manageable. Almost everything I say relates to my main idea.
- The reader will find many interesting and memorable moments here.
- I know quite a bit about this topic.
- Most of my details go beyond the obvious. The reader may gain some insight or learn one or two interesting things.

4
- The reader can tell what my main idea is. I may have a moment of confusing or vague writing. My paper is mostly focused.
- The reader will find some interesting and memorable moments here.
- If I knew more about this topic, the paper would be stronger.
- Some interesting or unusual details stand out. At other moments, I let my writing get too general, or I repeat things.

3
- The reader can guess what my main idea is. Some parts are not clear, though. I think it would help to make this topic smaller.
- The reader will find one or two interesting and memorable moments here.
- I need to know more about this topic to do a really good job. Sometimes I guessed or made things up.
- I have a few interesting details, but you have to hunt for them. A lot of this writing is general information everyone knows.

2
- My main idea is hard to figure out. I think a reader will wonder what it is I am trying to say. Maybe my topic is too big—or it's just unclear.
- I don't have any memorable moments here.
- I do not know much about my topic. Mostly I wrote to fill space.
- I need a lot more detail. This does not say much.

1
- I do not even *have* a main idea. I wrote whatever came into my head.
- I don't have any memorable moments here.
- I am still figuring out what I want to say. I'm just filling up the page until something comes to me.
- This is unclear and confusing. Most readers will not keep reading.

Recommended Literature for Teaching the Trait of Ideas

Ask students questions like these when you read all or part of a book: *What do you picture in your mind as you listen? Is this information clear? Did the writer use enough details to expand the topic?*

Anderson, Laurie Halse. 2000. *Fever 1793.* New York: Simon & Schuster. Factual and fictional details are skillfully used to create an intriguing plot with strong characters.

Claggett, Fran, Louann Reid, and Ruth Vinz. 1999. *Daybook of Critical Reading and Writing, Grade 8.* Wilmington, MA: Great Source. Literature excerpts combine with challenging writing tasks to touch on numerous skills related to the trait of ideas.

Hamm, Mia. 2000. *Go for the Goal: A Champion's Guide to Winning in Soccer and Life.* New York: HarperCollins. Hamm combines information with anecdotes.

Ibbotson, Eva. 2000. *Island of the Aunts.* New York: Dutton. Whimsical fantasy with delightful detail. Relatively easy reading with high interest level.

Irving, John. 2002. *A Prayer for Owen Meany.* New York: Random House. Strong sensory detail and vibrant imagery combine in one of Irving's best works.

Ryan, Pam Muñoz. 2000. *Esperanza Rising.* New York: Scholastic. Historically accurate, based on excellent research, and richly detailed.

Smith, Roland. 2000. *The Captain's Dog.* New York: Harcourt Books. The story is told from the dog's point of view, cleverly combining history with narrative.

Stegner, Wallace. 2000. *Wolf Willow.* New York: Penguin. Hauntingly beautiful coming of age story combining childhood memoir and adult reflections.

Sebranek, Patrick, Dave Kemper, and Verne Meyer. 1999. *Write Source 2000.* Wilmington, MA: Great Source. Information on gathering and identifying main ideas, using graphic organizers, and much more related to the trait of ideas.

More Ideas

Looking for more ideas on using literature to teach the trait of ideas? We recommend *Books, Lessons, Ideas for Teaching the Six Traits: Writing at Middle and High School,* published by Great Source. Compiled and annotated by Vicki Spandel. For information, please phone 800-289-4490.

Lesson 1 Will It Fit in My Backpack?

For use with pages 7–11 in the Student Traitbook

Starting with a topic that is too big is an invitation to disaster for most writers. They may try to tell everything and wind up overloading the text with details, anecdotes, facts, and illustrations—all in a well-intentioned effort to help the reader get the point.

Objectives

Students will gain skill in using the kind of probing questions that help a writer get at the smaller, more focused point he or she truly wishes to make.

Skills Focus

- Analyzing a sample for focus
- Designing probing questions that help narrow a broad topic
- Creating a topic sentence/thesis statement based on probing questions
- Analyzing personal writing to determine whether it is sufficiently focused and narrow

Time Frame

Allow about 45 minutes for this lesson. It can be divided into two parts. In Part 1 (25 minutes), ask students to read the sample from *Exploding Ants* (page 9 in the Student Traitbook) and discuss it with the class, focusing on the details. Also ask students to complete the "interview" with Dr. Settel and the brief chart of question words. In Part 2 (20 minutes), ask students to complete the personal conversation and create a topic sentence/thesis statement.

Setting Up the Lesson

Use Student Traitbook page 7 to introduce or review the trait of ideas. The Student Traitbook uses a backpack metaphor to illustrate the importance of keeping a topic narrow so that the writing does not become overloaded with details. You can illustrate this with a volunteer student, an empty backpack, and a stack of books. Ask the volunteer to put on the backpack, leaving it open so that you can place books in it. Then ask someone in the class to mention a broad topic. You may wish to jot down several possibilities, such as the world, the weather, people, and travel. Choose one of these topics. Then, ask students in the class to provide details related to this topic. (They should think of many!) Each time a student comes up with a detail, put a book in the backpack. Ask the volunteer to tell when the pack feels heavy enough—and when it begins to feel too heavy. Ask students whether they could add more details if they wished. They should say yes! Now, try the same thing with a smaller, more focused topic, such as things NOT to do when you're bathing a dog, what to do if you're caught outside in a thunderstorm, or annoying things people do while talking on the telephone. This time around the number of details should be much smaller.

Teaching the Lesson

Sharing an Example: *Exploding Ants*

Ask students to read the passage on their own and to underline at least three different things they learn about flukes. While analyzing the passage, students should agree that the topic is very narrow. Settel does not write about life forms in general or animals or small animals or even parasites. This is all about flukes and how they get inside the bodies of host animals. Spend some time comparing Settel's narrow topic to broader topics she might have used. Talk about how different the details might have been had she written about a broader topic, such as parasites.

From Probing Questions to Skinny Topics

The purpose of this portion of the lesson is to have students invent an imaginary interview they might have with Dr. Settel, author of *Exploding Ants.* Their role in the interview is to come up with questions that would help the author narrow her topic. The idea is to practice finding those questions that help a writer know whether his or her topic is too big or just right for the purpose. In the process, students should find themselves using some *who, what, which, where, when,* and *why* types of questions.

What Types of Questions?
Ask students to review each question they came up with in the imaginary interview. *How did each question begin? What types of question words seemed especially useful?* They should circle these in the Student Traitbook. You may wish to do a class tally to see which question words were used most often. This is also a good time to share two or three complete interviews aloud so that you can hear the various questions that students used. Talk about how questions can guide a writer to a smaller topic. Also share those questions that students think would have been most useful if this had been a real interview.

Narrowing the Topic
This time students will ask the questions and provide the answers—as if they were going to write about the topic "plants." This is a more difficult task than the preceding one. With the previous set of questions, students knew where the author was headed because they had already read Settel's passage on flukes. Invite them to be creative with their questions, following wherever the trail of questions leads. The only rule is to narrow the topic! At the end of this section, students should have a thesis statement and should be able to tell whether the topic "fits" within the scope of a research paper.

Extending the Lesson

- Propose a series of possible topics you might write about and ask students to help you evaluate each one. Is it narrow enough? If not, ask for their help in narrowing its scope. Make a list of their suggestions.
- Give students a chance to come up with big topics for one another. They should write them on index cards, put them all into a box, and then draw topics at random. The challenge is to reshape the big topics into something manageable and then share the results. You may want to post the results.
- "A Writer's Question" invites students to consider the outcome of an Internet search on the original topic "plants" and on narrowed versions of that topic. Try this with your students, and discuss the results. Be sure several students try the original topic, plants, and invite them to share the results. Compare their experience with those of other writers who began their searches with smaller topics. Which is easier to research, a big topic or a narrow one? Why? Can you use the Internet as a test of whether your topic is narrow enough?

Lesson 2

Setting the T-Table

For use with pages 12–15 in the Student Traitbook

In this lesson, students learn to use a tool called a T-Table to respond to a piece of literature and to do some prewriting. In using this tool, students learn that images (what they see in their minds) and reactions (emotional responses to the text) connect to the trait of ideas.

Objectives

Students will learn to use the T-Table to recognize strong imagery and to plan their own writing in a way that enriches ideas.

Skills Focus

- Analyzing writing to identify images that evoke feelings
- Comparing creative and informational writing in terms of what the reader sees and feels
- Creating a T-Table as a form of prewriting for a creative or informational piece

Time Frame

Allow about 60 minutes for this lesson. The lesson can be divided into two parts. In Part 1 (30 minutes), ask students to read the two examples from *Men of Stone* (page 12 in the Student Traitbook) and *Undaunted Courage* (page 13 in the Student Traitbook). In each case, students should fill out the T-Table. Provide time for students to discuss their responses in pairs and with the class. In Part 2 (30 minutes), ask each student to select a personal writing topic and design a T-Table for his or her personal writing.

Setting Up the Lesson

It is important in this lesson that students be able to separate images (what they see in their minds) from their feelings or other reactions to the text. To help them do this, choose an experience common to all (or most) of the students in your class, such as riding a roller coaster, visiting a shopping mall, or going into a dark movie theater. You need to choose something in which sensory experience plays a major role. Make a T-Table on the overhead transparency, and ask students to help you fill it in. On the left side, have them fill in images they see. On the right side, have them fill in their feelings or other reactions to those images. Point out that strong images, what the reader sees in his or her mind, help make ideas clear in a piece of writing; strong feelings give a written piece clarity (which is also a part of ideas, as the reader feels part of the writer's experience).

Teaching the Lesson

Sharing an Example: *Men of Stone*
Give students time to read this piece and to fill in the T-Table with whatever images and feelings come to mind. Encourage them to make at least three entries on each side. Also encourage them to read the text more than once. They should picture Mom shrugging and pouring coffee, Aunt Frieda's lined face, and the family gathered for some sort of conference. What a reader pictures in his or her mind does not always match the text exactly, so do not think of this as a memory quiz. The idea is to see what textual clues prompt a visual response. Students may have feelings of tension, curiosity, concern, anxiety, sadness (the funeral), or exasperation—just to mention a few possibilities. Give students time to compare responses with one another and as a class.

A Nonfiction Example:
Undaunted Courage
The purpose for this second example is to see what kinds of differences in imagery or feelings are elicited by a nonfiction piece. Though much informational writing is not intended to evoke personal feelings or reactions, some is. Again, ask students to read the sample (preferably twice) and respond by completing the T-Table. This time around, images they see might include the various people mentioned (Lincoln, Jefferson) and forms of transportation (steamboat, railroad). Some of the terminology in this informational piece is more abstract, such as *technology, gadgets, superior knowledge, advantages, society, transportation,* and *revolution.* These are not terms a reader can readily picture—and this is something you may wish to discuss once everyone has responded.

Reactions are likely to be different, as well. Informational writing can prompt a strong emotional response. Again, ask students to discuss their responses with a partner and then with the class as a whole. Some may find this table more difficult to fill out than the first.

Quick Share

Again, give students time to compare with partners and to discuss responses as a class.

Connecting to the Traits

Remind students that what they wrote on the "What I See" side of the T-Table is an indication of clear ideas. You may wish to compare the two samples, talking about how each writer makes ideas clear. Also remind students that the "What I Feel" side can connect to ideas, too, because readers can make personal connections to strong images. Did any of your students feel a sense of excitement or enthusiasm when reading the *Undaunted Courage* example? If so, this is a sign that the writer felt a real commitment to the topic and enjoyed writing it.

Your Turn to T-Off

It is time for students to create their own T-Tables. To do so, they will need to select a writing topic. Any topic will do. If students feel stuck, they can use the samples from the lesson as a resource for ideas. Encourage some students to try a nonfiction topic. Remind them that when they fill out the table, they should make short notes. As with their responses, they should aim for a minimum of three items on each side of the table. You might ask whether they believe the things listed in the T-Table are likely to change as they begin writing. (Most likely—yes!)

At the end of the activity, have students share T-Tables with partners. You may wish to ask for volunteers to share their examples aloud as well. Discuss the overall usefulness of the T-Table as a prewriting strategy. Would students be likely to use it again?

Extending the Lesson

- "A Writer's Question" asks students to think about using T-Tables to help guide revision. Discuss this with your class. Would this be useful? If so, how would the T-Table influence the revision a student does?
- Try a T-Table analysis of a piece of writing of the students' choice. What does the result show you about the strength of ideas in the piece you are analyzing?

Lesson 3 No Doubt About It

For use with pages 16–19 in the Student Traitbook

Readers do not appreciate doing all the work when it comes to making sense of a written text. It is the writer's job to make the message clear and to ensure that a piece of writing is understood by the reader without the writer being there to interpret, expand, or explain.

Objectives

Students will analyze a sample of professional writing for clarity and revise another to make sure it is clear enough to stand alone.

Skills Focus

- Analyzing a piece of professional writing to determine whether it is a stand-alone piece and to explore why it is or is not
- Identifying specific features of foggy writing
- Revising a short piece to transform it from foggy to clear and detailed

Time Frame

Allow about 45 minutes for this lesson, excluding any extensions. You can divide the lesson into two parts if you wish. In Part 1 (25 minutes), ask students to analyze the passage from *A Woolly Mammoth Journey* on page 16 in the Student Traitbook, complete the "Stand-Alone Writing" chart, discuss the chart with a partner, and complete the short response section called "Break It Down." In Part 2 (20 minutes), ask students to complete the section called "Leave No Doubt in Your Readers' Minds!" by revising the short paragraph on the Fourth of July fireworks and discussing the results with a partner.

Setting Up the Lesson

If you have some examples of foggy, nonspecific writing (e-mails, memos, tax codes, directions, and so on), this is a good time to use them to introduce the concept. If you do not have (or cannot find) a good example, make one up. Two or three sentences will do. Begin by reading the sample aloud. Then, ask students to rewrite the passage in their own words. If it's really foggy, they will find this difficult! If this task is too simple for them, it's a sign you haven't chosen a sufficiently vague sample. Once they have struggled a bit with the rewriting, ask whether they have any questions they would like to ask the writer (who might be you!). Read the piece aloud again, or show it on an overhead. Explain that in order to function well, writing needs to stand on its own; the writer cannot travel around with it to explain what does not make sense.

Teaching the Lesson

Sharing an Example: *A Woolly Mammoth Journey*

Read aloud the passage from Debbie S. Miller, or ask one of your students to read it. Remind students to look and listen for details about each of the mammoths and about the setting. What are they learning? Is it clear, or are they left with questions? Most should be able to picture the scene. Give them a few minutes to reread the passage and to underline details or make notes in the margins.

Stand-Alone Writing

When writing makes sense, it should be fairly easy to notice specific details that aid the reader's understanding. Give students a few minutes to complete the chart, writing just two or three details about each of the woolly mammoths, the setting, and mammoth behavior in general. Students should also respond to the questions about Miller's writing: Does she create a clear picture? (Most should say yes.) Does this writing stand alone? (Most students should agree that it does.)

Share and Compare

Invite students to share their responses, compare notes, and then discuss ideas as a class. Most should agree that Miller creates a clear picture of the landscape within which the mammoths lived as well as the mammoths themselves.

Break It Down

In this part of the lesson, students are asked to analyze a foggy version of Miller's original. Though student assessors may not check all of the items listed here, it is possible to do so and to defend them all. The example is vague and provides no specific information about mammoths. Reinforce the notion that good detail goes beyond casual observation; it should teach the reader or create a vivid impression—or both.

Leave No Doubt in Your Readers' Minds!

Ask students to rewrite the piece on the Fourth of July fireworks so that it is a sample of stand-alone writing. You may wish to do a revision of your own to share with students. Here is a suggested revision.

This year our neighbors spent hundreds of dollars on fireworks. They went for noise and color, buying the loudest, most high-flying fireworks available. The show started around 10, and from then until midnight our street was ablaze with booming, sparkling explosions of blue, purple, orange, gold, and green light. No one could hear their televisions. My dog Peaches hid under the bed, covering her ears. I felt like doing the same. Since these people don't know the meaning of the word "caution," I was fearful something would catch on fire—and sure enough, it did.

Extending the Lesson

- Ask each student to look at an in-process sample of his or her own work to see whether it is specific and adequately detailed or whether some revision is needed. They should revise as necessary to remove all fogginess from the writing.
- Send students on a foggy writing search. Tell them to find examples of vague nonspecific writing. Give a "Foggy"—an award for the most vague, unclear writing anyone can find. Revise one or more of the samples with the students if you wish.
- Where do students' favorite authors fit on the foggy-to-stand-alone continuum? Ask students to search for some specific passages and analyze them for stand-alone quality. If their examples are strong, each should have the four features listed in the section marked "Break It Down." Remind students that they can use this same checklist to make sure their own writing is of stand-alone quality.

Lesson 4

Just Right

For use with pages 20–23 in the Student Traitbook

Specific, interesting details are good for readers. Detail overload (also known as filler) simply weighs a reader down, overwhelming him or her with more information than is necessary. This lesson gives students some practice in striking a balance between nonspecific writing and detail overload.

Objectives

Students will learn to recognize filler and then to eliminate it to make writing more concise and interesting.

Skills Focus

- Understanding the concept of "filler"
- Analyzing a sample of professional writing to see whether it contains filler
- Revising to eliminate filler from writing

Time Frame

Allow about 35 minutes for this lesson, excluding any extensions.

Setting Up the Lesson

Filler is the writing equivalent of excess baggage. It's noticeable in speaking, as well. You can illustrate this by what you say at the beginning of class: *Good morning on this beautiful (DAY) in (MONTH), and welcome to our usual classroom of (COLOR) walls with (NUMBER OF) students, seated at (NUMBER OF TABLES/DESKS) where they listen, read, write, take notes, and do other work. I will be your teacher again today as I am on other days, having made a career of teaching, a profession I enjoy, and you will continue to be the students. As your teacher, I will be giving you some directions about what to do for today's lesson, which will be about writing, or conveying ideas in written form to an audience . . .* and so on. Ask students what they notice about the ridiculous way you are speaking. At least one should notice you are saying a whole lot more than anyone needs to hear. Now, while you're working on getting your wild speech under control, they'll be working to get rid of filler in *writing*—but you'll begin with an example that's mostly filler-free (we think).

Teaching the Lesson

Sharing an Example: *Artemis Fowl*
Ask students to listen carefully as you read aloud the excerpt from Eoin Colfer's book *Artemis Fowl.* (Or, ask students to read it on their own.) They should listen for details about Artemis and the world in which he lives. Does the writer tell enough to satisfy readers? Does he tell too much? Most students should feel Colfer strikes a good balance by letting the reader picture Artemis and his surroundings but also providing some hints about what he is trying to do.

What Did You Find Out?
To complete this graphic, students should analyze their personal responses to the passage from *Artemis Fowl.* Inside the box, each student should list five (or more) things he or she learned from the passage. Outside the box, students should list any items they consider filler. Many students may have no "filler" items at all, and that's fine. If they do, talk about why they categorized them as filler. It may be helpful for them to reread the passage, rechecking the details and comparing the passage to their graphic analyses.

What If?
In this part of the lesson, students will see a passage with filler crossed out. It is helpful also to hear it, however. Read the passage aloud, including the deleted filler, so that students can use both their eyes and ears to experience the full impact of overloaded writing. Discuss personal responses. If all writing were like this, would people want to read? Do your students agree that the crossed-out passages weaken

the piece by adding detail overload? Do any of them like the extra information? If so, why?

Crossing Out Filler

This time around, students have an opportunity to do the cutting themselves. The sample passage about a neighborhood Fourth of July celebration is loaded with filler. Encourage students to be rigorous and to cut what is not needed. Tell students that it is all right to add a word or a phrase or to change the structure of a sentence if necessary. Make sure each student works individually before comparing changes with a partner. Later, partners can check to see whether they made the same corrections. Edit the passage yourself so that you can compare your version to students' versions. Here is one possible revision, which is one-half the length of the original:

The people in our neighborhood must have been feeling especially patriotic this year because I've never seen or heard so many fireworks on the Fourth of July. Once the sun set, it sounded like a war zone. Our neighbors always buy a huge arsenal of everything that sparks, whistles, flames, and booms. Last year, the little boy who lives across the street spent the whole day indoors because the noise freaked him out. This year, he announced, "I'm four. I like fireworks now."

Share and Compare

As you share revisions, talk about how much of the original has been cut. Student writers may not cut quite as much as was cut in the example, but they should cut at least one-fourth to one-third of the original. If most of your students do not meet this goal, suggest that they work with partners to have one more look.

Extending the Lesson

- Ask each student to review one or more pieces of his or her own writing. How would students rate themselves in terms of the amount of filler they find? Did they overdo it? Or did they strike a good balance with just the right amount of detail?
- Analyze some writing from various sources, such as textbooks, menus, newspapers, journals, e-mail, or advertisements. Which examples contain the most filler, and which ones are more filler free? Are certain types of writing more likely to have filler than others? Why is this?
- Have students create their own lessons by intentionally writing some detail-overloaded pieces. To do this, students can begin with a balanced piece of writing and then add unnecessary details. Then, have them exchange papers with partners and revise to cut the filler. Compare students' revisions to the originals. Did they find the balance the original author intended?

Ideas

Teacher's Guide pages 5, 120–131
Transparency numbers 1–4

Objective

Students will review and apply what they have learned about the trait of ideas.

Reviewing Ideas

Review with students what they have learned about the trait of ideas. Ask students to discuss what ideas are and to explain why ideas are important in a piece of writing. Then ask them to recall the main points about ideas that are discussed in Unit 1. Students' responses should include the following points:

- Narrow the topic by giving it focus.
- Use a T-Table prewriting strategy that enhances both ideas and voice.
- Transform fuzzy writing into clear, stand-alone text.
- Eliminate the filler that confuses and distracts readers.

Applying Ideas

To help students apply what they have learned about the trait of ideas, distribute copies of the Student Rubric for Ideas on page 5 of this Teacher's Guide. Students will use the rubric to score one or more of the sample papers that begin on page 116. The papers for ideas are also on overhead transparencies 1–4.

Before students score the papers, explain that a rubric is a grading system that determines the score a piece of writing should receive for a particular trait. Preview the Student Rubric for Ideas, pointing out that a paper very strong in ideas receives a score of 6 and a paper very weak in ideas receives a score of 1. Tell students to read the rubric and then read the paper they will score. Then tell them to look at the paper and the rubric together to determine the score the paper should receive. Encourage students to make notes on each paper to help them score it. For example, they might place a check mark next to fuzzy writing.

Overview

This unit focuses on organization—putting information into an order that makes sense and holds a reader's attention from beginning to end. Students will practice identifying patterns that match the content and purpose of a topic, building connections between ideas by using strong transitions, and putting all the elements of sound organization together in an original piece of writing.

The focus of instruction in this unit will be

- identifying patterns that make for strong organization
- finding the right pattern to match topic and purpose
- using transitions to build connections between ideas
- putting all organizational strategies together to create a piece that is easy for readers to follow and understand

Organization: *A Definition*

Organization is the internal structure in a piece of writing. That structure gives ideas direction, purpose, and momentum. Good organization holds writing together, making it easy for readers to see the big picture. Several things make organization work well: a *lead* that catches readers' attention, an *organizational sequence* that makes ideas easy to follow, a clear and sustained *focus* on the main idea (no wandering!), strong *transitions* that link the writer's ideas together, and an appropriate *conclusion* that effectively wraps things up.

The Unit at a Glance

The following lessons in the Teacher's Guide and practice exercises in the Student Traitbook will help develop understanding of the trait of organization. The Unit Summary provides an opportunity to practice evaluating papers for organization.

Unit Introduction: Organization

Teacher's Guide pages 20–24	The unique features of organization are presented along with rubrics and a list of recommended literature for teaching organization.

Lesson 5: Looking for a Pattern

Teacher's Guide pages 25–27 ***Student Traitbook pages 24–28***	In this lesson, students work with five organizational patterns, focusing on matching pattern with purpose.

Lesson 6: Finding the Perfect Match

Teacher's Guide pages 28–30 ***Student Traitbook pages 29–32***	This lesson expands the concepts and strategies practiced in Lesson 5, introducing students to three additional organizational patterns and offering further practice in finding the pattern that best showcases the writer's message.

Lesson 7: Clear Connections

Teacher's Guide pages 31–33 ***Student Traitbook pages 33–36***	Writing that lacks strong transitions can leave readers feeling disconnected. In this lesson, students learn to identify good transitions and to revise writing to make transitions stronger.

Lesson 8: Creating the Total Package

Teacher's Guide pages 34–36 ***Student Traitbook pages 37–40***	A strong, clear message isn't enough by itself. Words, sentences, and concepts need structure to create meaning. In this lesson, each student uses organizational strategies to create an original piece of writing.

Unit Summary: Organization

Teacher's Guide page 37 ***Overhead numbers 5–8***	Use the student rubric on page 23 and the activities in the Summary to practice assessing writing for the trait of organization. Five-point rubrics, along with rationales for scores on sample papers, appear in the Appendix of this Teacher's Guide, pages 192–213.

Teacher Rubric for Organization

6
- The writer focuses on the main message throughout the paper.
- The organizational pattern is perfect for the topic, purpose, and audience; it enhances the reader's understanding of the text.
- Transitions are smooth, clearly connecting sentences and ideas to create a coherent whole.
- The opening is strong and compelling, and the conclusion is thoroughly satisfying.

5
- The writer seldom wanders from the main point.
- The organizational pattern fits the topic, purpose, and audience.
- Transitions adequately connect ideas.
- The opening is appealing and the ending works.

4
- The writer does not always focus on the main idea, but this is not distracting or confusing.
- The organizational pattern works for the most part.
- Transitions are present, but the writer has to make *some* connections.
- The opening and closing are functional, if not original.

3
- The writer wanders from the main point enough to create some confusion.
- The organizational pattern may not match the task well; it may be too formulaic, or simply hard to follow.
- Transitions are sometimes present, sometimes not.
- The opening and closing are present; one or both need work.

2
- Lack of order frequently leaves the reader feeling lost.
- The pattern is so formulaic it's distracting—or there is no pattern.
- Transitions are rarely attempted.
- The opening and closing are either missing or need a lot of work.

1
- The text is basically a disjointed collection of random thoughts.
- There is no identifiable structure/pattern. It's impossible to follow.
- Transitions are absent. Ideas do not seem connected.
- There is no real opening or closing.

Student Rubric for Organization

6
- I stick with one topic. I never wander.
- I chose an organizational pattern that fits my topic, purpose, and audience very well. This pattern helps make my meaning clear.
- My transitions build strong bridges from sentence to sentence, from idea to idea.
- My opening will grab your attention; my ending brings the paper to closure and leaves you thinking.

5
- I stick with one topic—well most of the time!
- My organizational pattern fits my topic, purpose, and audience.
- Most of my transitions work.
- My opening leads the reader into the paper, and my ending wraps up main points quite effectively.

4
- I might have wandered a *little* from my main topic—but I got back on track.
- I have an organizational pattern. I think it fits the task OK.
- I used some transitions, but the reader needs to make some connections.
- My opening goes with the rest of my paper; my ending lets the reader know the paper is finished.

3
- I wandered from my main topic now and then.
- I tried to follow an organizational pattern. I'm not sure it fits my purpose.
- I thought about transitions, but the reader needs to make a lot of connections.
- I have a lead and a conclusion, but they both need work.

2
- I wrote about too many things. I forgot what my main topic was.
- I do not think there is a pattern here. This is more like a messy closet!
- I might have one or two transitions, but I'm not sure they connect things clearly.
- I think I forgot to write a lead, and I think I forgot my ending, too. It just stops. Maybe I wrote "The End" . . .

1
- This doesn't make any sense. I don't even *have* a main topic yet!
- Pattern? Are you kidding? Nothing goes with anything else.
- How could I have transitions when nothing goes with anything else?
- There is no lead or conclusion.

Recommended Books for Teaching Organization

Use excerpts from these books or from your favorites to model organizational structures, transitions, leads, and conclusions.

Claggett, Fran, Louann Reid, and Ruth Vinz. 1999. *Daybook of Critical Reading and Writing, Grade 8.* Wilmington, MA: Great Source. Excerpts from literature combine with writing tasks that touch on organization-related skills: for example, organizing through cause-and-effect patterns, comparing ideas, linking main idea and detail effectively, and much more.

Bauer, Joan. *Backwater.* 1999. New York: Penguin Putnam. Excellent chapter leads and conclusions help build suspense in a tightly knit story.

Cather, Willa. *My Antonia.* 1995. New York: Houghton Mifflin. Organized into "books" or chunks of the narrator's life, versus an "every moment" account.

Fleischman, Paul. *Seedfolks.* 1997. New York: HarperCollins. Thirteen chapters with thirteen memorable voices combine to weave a tale of understanding and respect.

Gallo, Donald R., editor. *Time Capsule: Short Stories About Teenagers Throughout the Twentieth Century.* 1999. New York: Random House. Decade by decade, main events are juxtaposed with life as teens experienced it then.

Ingold, Jeanette. *The Big Burn.* 2002. San Diego: Harcourt. Based on the true story of one of the biggest wildfires of the twentieth century, this story is told in journal form.

Jimenez, Francisco. *The Circuit.* 1997. Albuquerque: University of New Mexico Press. Independent but closely intertwined stories of a migrant family as they move from one labor camp to another.

Johnson, Angela. *Looking for Red.* 2002. New York: Simon and Schuster. Spare, haunting prose recounts the story of a young adolescent who mourns her drowned brother.

Orlev, Uri. *The Island on Bird Street.* 1984. Boston: Houghton Mifflin. Each fascinating chapter brings a new problem to solve—and a new ingenious solution.

Paulsen, Gary. *The Rifle.* 1995. New York: Harcourt Brace. Extremely powerful, with unforgettable leads, conclusions, and historical transitions.

Van Draanen, Wendelin. *Flipped.* 2001. New York: Knopf. In alternating chapters, eighth graders Bryce and Juli describe how they have changed from when they met in second grade.

Lesson 5 Looking for a Pattern

For use with pages 24–28 in the Student Traitbook

There are many ways to organize information in a piece of writing. The "best" choice depends on content, purpose, and audience. The author of a mystery story may deliberately withhold information, but the writer of a news story wants to get all the facts to the reader as quickly as possible. This lesson is about matching the organizational pattern with the purpose to create effective writing.

Objectives

Students will review and discuss five organizational patterns, identify various patterns in samples of writing, and use one pattern to create an original piece on a personally selected topic.

Skills Focus

- Understanding five key organizational patterns
- Recognizing various patterns within samples of writing
- Selecting an appropriate pattern to fit an original piece of writing

Time Frame

Allow about 50 minutes for this lesson. The lesson can be divided into two parts if you wish. In Part 1 (20 minutes), ask students to review the five organizational patterns under "A Palette of Patterns" and to identify those they have used in their own writing. They should also read the three samples under "Pick a Pattern, Please" and match each to one of the five patterns listed. In Part 2 (30 minutes), students should write a short piece, using one of the five patterns.

Setting Up the Lesson

Introduce or review the concept of organization, using page 24 in the Student Traitbook.

Ask students how many ways they can think of to organize writing. Before they look at this lesson, have students brainstorm a list to see how many ways they can name. They should think of at least six or eight, many of which they're likely to encounter in this lesson. If they get stuck, ask them to look at their own writing or any other sources for possible patterns. Later, you can compare the patterns listed in this lesson with students' original list.

> *"Invention is a form of organization."*
>
> —Graham Greene

Teaching the Lesson

A Palette of Patterns

Go through this short list with students, pattern by pattern. Make sure that everyone understands how each pattern works. Ask them to check off those patterns that they have used before, and see who can recall a sample of each from their own reading—whether in school or otherwise. Share samples of your own as well. Which pattern is most popular? Most students will likely say *chronological order* or *order of importance.* Emphasize that this means most writing should fit one of these patterns. Although some ways of organizing information are more comfortable to many of us, possibilities for organizing any piece of writing are numerous.

Pick a Pattern, Please

In this section of the lesson, students are asked to carefully read three samples and to identify the pattern (from the list of five) the author has used. They should work individually first and then compare results with partners. Be sure to discuss any disagreements. Suggested responses follow.

Sample 1

Cause and Effect; the lightning storm has caused an electrical outage at the swimming pool.

Sample 2
Comparison; the author compares the weather in Nebraska with that in Arizona.

Sample 3
Order of Location (sometimes called "visual organization"); the author describes the scene as it unfolds.

Following a Pattern
For this closing section, each student should select a personal topic and create an original piece of writing (at least eight sentences or longer) that follows one of the five organizational patterns discussed in the lesson.

Extending the Lesson

- Invite students to review their own writing and to identify organizational patterns. Make a class summary of the results. How many different patterns are students using?
- Ask students to share their writing from this lesson in small groups. Prior to sharing, have each writer keep secret the pattern being used. See whether others in the group can correctly identify this pattern. If they cannot, does the writer need to make the pattern clearer? Do responders need to work on their listening skills?
- Share a sample of your own writing, and ask students to identify the pattern they hear. Can they identify it? If not, is it their listening—or is it your writing?
- Do these patterns fit poetry as well as prose? Read a few samples of poetry to find out. Do students notice organizational patterns? Might patterns be slightly different for poetry? Why?

Lesson 6

Finding the Perfect Match

For use with pages 29–32 in the Student Traitbook

In writing, a good match between purpose and pattern is essential. If a recipe, for example, were written as a mystery story ("Guess the Secret Ingredient!"), it might make entertaining reading but lousy lemon pie. This lesson reinforces the importance of ensuring that purpose and pattern match well.

Objectives

In this lesson, students match pattern to purpose by exploring three additional organizational patterns, matching them to a purpose, and using one of the identified patterns to create an original piece.

Skills Focus

- Understanding eight organizational patterns
- Matching hypothetical samples of writing to the appropriate pattern
- Creating an original piece of writing that uses one of the eight patterns discussed

Time Frame

Allow about 50 minutes for this lesson. It can be divided into two parts. In Part 1 (20 minutes), ask students to review and respond to the list of eight organizational patterns under "Eight Eligible Candidates." They should also match one of these eight patterns to each of the hypothetical writing tasks under "Write a Match for It." In Part 2 (30 minutes), students should create an original piece of writing that focuses on the theme "games."

Setting Up the Lesson

Create three short writing samples, each on the same topic, to show how the organizational structure of a piece affects purpose and reader response. For example, what if a recipe were written as a cause-and-effect piece? What if it were written as a comparison piece? Now try it as a step-by-step piece. Read all three samples aloud, and ask students for their responses. Does a good match between purpose and pattern make writing easier to follow and understand?

Teaching the Lesson

Eight Eligible Candidates

Students should be familiar with five of the eight patterns listed here from the previous lesson. This time around, as they review each, ask them to put a check mark next to each pattern they have used *within the last month.* If possible, they should try to recall what sort of writing fit each pattern. Discuss results with the class as a whole. Which patterns were used most often and on which types of writing? Were any patterns not used by anyone at all? If so, why might that be? Discuss any patterns students would not feel comfortable using or do not understand.

Write a Match for It

In this portion of the lesson, students should match each of the hypothetical writing tasks listed to the pattern that seems most appropriate. It is possible that more than one pattern could fit some samples, depending on an author's approach. Here are some suggested matches:

1. How to change a flat tire
   Step-by-Step
2. Article about the new principal
   Main Events
3. Editorial on changing the school's mascot and team names
   Point and Counterpoint
4. Journal entries on the trip to Washington, D.C.
   Chronological Order
5. Aerial description of Mount St. Helens
   Order of Location (Spatial)
6. Editorial on two contenders for a film award
   Point and Counterpoint OR Comparison
7. Voter's pamphlet explaining why you should vote for a sales tax
   Point and Counterpoint OR Order of Importance

Share and Compare

Encourage students to offer reasons for their selections as they share. For any given piece, more than one organizational approach is likely to fit. In some cases, a writer may combine organizational approaches. Stress the point that making a good match does not mean locking yourself into a single approach.

Pattern Practice
In this closing portion of the lesson, students should create an original piece of writing on the theme "games" that matches one of the organizational patterns described. Students can interpret the word "games" in any way and can use any form of writing from a how-to or step-by-step account to a story, an essay, or a persuasive piece. The important thing is for each student to have a clear sense of what his or her message will be and to know which organizational pattern he or she will use.

Extending the Lesson

- Review the list of seven hypothetical writing tasks under "Write a Match for It." Could any or all of these tasks be organized in a different way from the one(s) students first identified? How does shifting the pattern shift the purpose?
- Invite students to share their practice writing from "Pattern Practice" in small groups and to see whether listeners can identify the pattern without a hint from the writer. Discuss results.
- As the class reads (novels, short stories, poems, articles) over the next month or so, keep track of the organizational patterns they identify. Do most patterns fit within this list of eight? Can students also identify some new patterns?

Lesson 7

Clear Connections

For use with pages 33–36 in the Student Traitbook

Anyone who has made a telephone call and received a weak connection knows how frustrating that experience can be. Weak connections in writing can be frustrating, too. When a writer fails to link thoughts or sentences together, the reader must do it. Unfortunately, unlike callers, writers seldom "phone back."

Objectives

Students learn the value of transitions and gain practice in both identifying transitional phrases and using them in their own writing.

Skills Focus

- Understanding the concept of "transition"
- Identifying transitional words or phrases in a piece of writing
- Revising a piece with weak or missing transitions to make those transitions stronger

Time Frame

Allow about 55 minutes for this lesson, excluding any extensions. You can divide the lesson into two parts. In Part 1 (25 minutes), ask students to analyze the passage by Ji Li Jiang, paying particular attention to the highlighted transitions. Also, take time to review and discuss the list of transitional words and phrases in the Student Traitbook. Ask students to underline the transitions they find in the passage from *Orvis*. In Part 2 of the lesson (30 minutes), give students an opportunity to revise the passage under "Creating a Strong Connection," improving the transitional words and phrases used in the original.

Setting Up the Lesson

Students need to understand that a transition is any word or phrase that links two ideas or two sentences. Start with a sample of a transitional word or phrase used effectively.

Jennifer was an incredibly fast runner. Therefore, she won many races.

Now, try two sentences in which you omit the transition and invite students to fill it in. One possibility is given.

The fire approached our neighborhood. We did not anticipate any evacuation.

The fire approached our neighborhood. Nevertheless, we did not anticipate any evacuation.

Insert a transitional word or phrase that does not work. For example, *moreover* suggests emphasis when in fact a cause-and-effect relationship is called for. Students should suggest a transition word such as *therefore.*

Don was deathly afraid of horses. Moreover, when Sue suggested riding, he asked whether they could go river rafting instead.

Teaching the Lesson

Sharing an Example: *Red Scarf Girl*

Ask students to read the passage from Ji Li Jiang's memoir *Red Scarf Girl* (pages 33–34 of the Student Traitbook). Remind them to pay particular attention to the transitional words and phrases highlighted in colored print. Ask whether they think these transitional phrases are helpful in connecting the ideas. To illustrate the difference, read aloud this revision of the first few lines from Ji Li Jiang's original passage.

I remembered coming home from kindergarten, showing Grandma songs and dances. Grandma sat with her knitting, nodding in time to the music. There was singing with an unsteady pitch and a heavy Tianjin accent. A head was wagging. Arms were moving.

Words That Connect

After discussing the *Red Scarf Girl* passage, look carefully at the list of transitional words. Explain that this list does not represent all transitions. Pronouns are often used as transitions: *George dreaded math. It was his toughest subject—next to English, art, history, and PE.* In this example, we know *It* refers to *math;* the use of a simple pronoun connects the two sentences for us. Reinforce the idea that a transition is any word or phrase that links two ideas or two sentences.

A Little Practice

This time around, students must spot the transitions for themselves. Read the passage from *Orvis* aloud if you feel this will be helpful for students. Following are the transitional words and phrases:

With Orvis's instructions and the glass shard for a knife, More than an hour, By that time, Leaving Orvis to turn the spit, until they, but, this, his, When, and it's.

Share and Compare
Did most students agree on which words or phrases served as transitions? Did students mark transitions that were not marked on the sample?

Creating a Strong Connection
This passage about the county fair suffers from weak, overdone, and inappropriate transitions. Students should feel free to rewrite sentences, changing the wording as necessary to make new transitions read more smoothly. Following is a *suggested* revision with changes marked in boldfaced type.

Our county fair has this really strange event that combines a couple of traditional fair activities. ~~**For this reason,**~~ It's known as the pig and Ford races. ~~**Beyond this event**~~ **For** this event, they release a whole bunch of greased pigs as the contestants are standing by their vehicles—old hand-cranked Ford flatbed trucks. ~~**Later**~~ **To kick things off,** the starter fires his gun, ~~**so**~~ **and** the contestants run around and try to grab hold of one of the pigs. ~~**In the same way,**~~ Anyone who can catch a pig carries it to his or her truck before trying to crank-start the truck. ~~**To repeat,**~~ When the trucks are running, drivers have to guide them beneath the arena to the finish line. **As a reward,** the winner ~~**afterward**~~ gets to keep the pig.

Extending the Lesson

- Invite students to look at writing from their own folders. Using the list from pages 34–35 in the Student Traitbook and what they have learned from this lesson, invite them to identify transitions in their writing and revise where transitions are weak, inappropriate, or missing.

Lesson 8

Creating the Total Package

For use with pages 37–40 in the Student Traitbook

Writing that contains good organization includes an interesting lead, details in an effective order, sound transitions, and a thoughtful conclusion. Eventually, all these pieces and parts must come together to form a solid, well-organized piece of writing.

Objectives

Each student will write a paper about earthquakes that includes a strong lead, details in an effective order, thoughtful transitions, and a strong conclusion.

Skills Focus

- Selecting quality details from a list
- Identifying a main idea
- Identifying an organizational pattern that fits the main idea
- Writing a strong lead based on a particularly intriguing detail
- Writing a strong conclusion
- Analyzing personal writing for its strengths and weaknesses in organization

Time Frame

Allow about 65 minutes for this lesson, excluding any extensions.

Setting Up the Lesson

Brainstorm an "Enemies of Good Organization" checklist that students can refer to as they write their paragraphs on earthquakes. Encourage them to think of what they've learned in previous lessons and also to use their own experiences in creating a personal checklist. They should use their own words and try to think of things that truly get in the way of good organization, such as getting off to a slow start with a weak lead, having a hard time focusing on a main topic (or not knowing what it is), trying to tell too much, hurrying when writing the conclusion, or forgetting to show the reader how ideas connect. Post the class checklist where everyone can see it, and add to it as you go if necessary.

Teaching the Lesson

A Smart Shopper

As students read through the list of details on earthquakes, encourage them to look for what is most interesting or important. They should eliminate anything that is general, redundant, or common knowledge. This activity is best done individually because students are not likely to agree completely on which details are "keepers." Encourage students to limit the number of keepers to 10 or fewer. Students with firsthand knowledge of this topic may wish to add one or two details of their own. Writers who try to include too many details may have difficulty maintaining focus. On the other hand, writers who select fewer than eight details may not have enough information to fill a strong paragraph.

What's in Your MFT Cart?

Ask students to review their lists. Did they overload their "shopping carts"? Do they have enough information? They should also check to see whether the separate bits of information they have chosen seem to go together.

Bringing It into Focus

Organization depends on focus—and focus depends on having a main message to convey. Students should look carefully at the details they identified as keepers. What do these details have in common? Is there a theme—or main idea—that holds those details together? **HINT:** "All About Earthquakes" is not a main idea; it's only a topic in search of a main idea. Main ideas can be put into sentence form, like this:

- *We use technology to protect ourselves from earthquakes.*
- *Few people realize just how destructive earthquakes can be.*

Remind students that identifying a strong main idea makes every other part of organizing information easier—from deleting unneeded information to writing a lead to wrapping things up.

What's the Pattern?
After students have identified a main idea, they should have little difficulty coming up with a pattern to match. Remind students to look in Lesson 6 if they cannot easily recall the many patterns available. The point is to think about a possible direction the paper could (or should) take.

Off to a Hot Start
This portion of the lesson offers students an opportunity to write a strong lead. One good strategy for doing this is to review the list of informational items they put in their "shopping carts." The most startling or striking bit of information often translates into a dynamite lead. And—as with any component of writing—the lead can always be changed later. **TIP:** A good lead often produces strong writing. Encourage students to avoid lazy, placeholder leads like these:

- Earthquakes are interesting.
- This will be a paper about earthquakes.
- In this paper I will explain why earthquakes are dangerous.

Keep the Energy Flowing
Students who worked hard on their leads should ease right into this part of the lesson. The less time spent coming up with a good lead, the harder this portion of the writing will be. Students' papers should be at least eight sentences in length. Their main objectives are these:

- Making the main message stand out
- Using an organizational pattern that fits the purpose of the writing
- Ensuring that the lead is captivating and strong
- Using good transitions to link ideas
- Writing a conclusion that wraps things up nicely

Extending the Lesson

- Wait two or three days and then have students revise their paragraphs on earthquakes to make them even stronger in organization.
- Brainstorm some of the strategies students used to revise for organization, such as rewriting the lead, refining the main idea, finding a different organizational pattern, excluding information that was not relevant, adding or strengthening transitions, or rewriting the conclusion.
- Compare this piece of writing with others students have done. Do students consider their earthquake papers stronger in organization? If so, how much did it help to have a systematic process for setting up the paper?

Organization

Teacher's Guide pages 23, 132–143
Transparency numbers 5–8

Objective

Students will review and apply what they have learned about the trait of organization.

Reviewing Organization

Review with students what they have learned about the trait of organization. Ask students to discuss what organization means and to explain why it is important in a piece of writing. Then ask them to recall the main points about organization that are discussed in Unit 2. Students' responses should include the following points:

- Identify patterns that make for strong organization.
- Find the right pattern to match topic and purpose.
- Use transitions to build strong connections between sentences and ideas.

Applying Organization

To help students apply what they have learned about the trait of organization, distribute copies of the Student Rubric for Organization on page 23 of this Teacher's Guide. Students will use the rubric to score one or more of the sample papers that begin on page 116. The papers for organization are also on overhead transparencies 5–8.

Before students score the papers, explain that a rubric is a grading system that determines the score a piece of writing should receive for a particular trait. Preview the Student Rubric for Organization, pointing out that a paper very strong in organization receives a score of 6 and a paper very weak in organization receives a score of 1. Tell students to read the rubric and then read the paper they will score. Then tell them to look at the paper and the rubric together to determine the score the paper should receive. Encourage students to make notes on each paper to help them score it. For example, they might underline effective transition words or phrases.

Overview

This unit focuses on voice, a trait that reflects individuality and personality. Voice comes from a skillful blend of detail and word choice, enthusiasm for and knowledge of the topic, and attention to audience. As students will discover, voice is among the most valuable tools a writer can use to seize and hold the attention of an audience and, ultimately, to enhance the message.

The focus of instruction in this unit will be

- helping students create a personal definition for the trait of voice
- using voice to keep readers "connected" to an informational topic
- matching voice to audience
- revising to energize, voiceless writing

Voice: *A Definition*

Voice is the quality that keeps readers reading. It's the way a writer uses his or her individual style, tone, and perspective on the world to make the message clear and appealing. As one teacher put it, your *ideas* are what you have to say; your *voice* is how you say it. Students need to understand that voice changes as the audience changes; the voice of a business letter is not the voice of a spine-tingling narrative about mountain climbing. Voice is also a reflection of confidence—confidence that can only come from knowing a topic well. It is sometimes suggested that informational or expository writing has little voice. We disagree. It simply has a different *kind* of voice.

The Unit at a Glance

The following lessons in the Teacher's Guide and practice exercises in the Student Traitbook will help develop understanding of the trait of voice. The Unit Summary provides an opportunity to practice evaluating papers for voice.

Unit Overview: Voice

Teacher's Guide pages 38–42 — The unique features of the trait of voice are presented along with a rubric and a list of recommended literature for teaching voice.

Lesson 9: A Defining Moment

Teacher's Guide pages 43–45
Student Traitbook pages 41–45

In this lesson, students develop a personal definition of voice that they can use in assessing their own writing.

Lesson 10: Keeping Readers Connected

Teacher's Guide pages 46–48
Student Traitbook pages 46–49

In this lesson, students practice ways of building reader connections by sharing knowledge and projecting confidence in informational writing.

Lesson 11: Thinking About Audience

Teacher's Guide pages 49–51
Student Traitbook pages 50–53

In this lesson, students practice matching voice to the needs and expectations of an audience.

Lesson 12: Kick It into High Gear!

Teacher's Guide pages 52–54
Student Traitbook pages 54–57

In this lesson, students explore their personal responses to a piece of writing and then use what they have learned to revise a passage that is low on "voice fuel."

Unit Summary: Voice

Teacher's Guide page 55
Overhead numbers 9–12

Use the student rubric on page 41 and the activities in the Summary to practice assessing writing for the trait of voice. Remember that 5-point rubrics, along with rationales for scores on sample papers, appear in the Appendix of this Teacher's Guide, pages 192–213.

Teacher Rubric for Voice

6
- This writing is as individual as fingerprints. If you know the writer, you can identify him or her readily.
- The reader will feel compelled to share the piece aloud.
- It is lively, energetic, and hard to put down. It explodes with energy.
- The voice is carefully selected to fit the purpose and audience perfectly.

5
- This paper stands out from others. It may be recognizable if you know the writer.
- The reader would probably share this piece aloud.
- It shows strong feelings and is appealing to read. It has a lot of energy.
- The voice is suitable for the audience and purpose.

4
- This voice is distinctive, though not unique.
- The reader might share parts of this piece aloud.
- Moments of passion, energy, or strong feelings are evident throughout.
- The voice is acceptable for the audience and purpose but could use refining.

3
- This is a functional, sincere voice, though not especially distinctive.
- The piece does not seem quite ready to share aloud.
- Moments of passion, energy, or strong feelings are rare. You need to look.
- The voice may or may not seem acceptable for the purpose or audience.

2
- This is an anybody kind of voice.
- The piece is definitely not ready to share aloud.
- This writing could use a serious energy boost. The writer sounds bored.
- The voice is very faint or not a good match for audience and purpose.

1
- This voice is difficult to identify or describe—or it's the *wrong* voice for the writing task.
- Lack of voice makes this a piece the reader would *not* share aloud.
- No energy or excitement over the topic comes through.
- The voice is missing or wholly inappropriate for the audience and purpose.

Student Rubric for Voice

6
- This paper is so distinctive; you can tell at once that it's MY voice.
- I think you will definitely want to share this paper aloud.
- I LOVE this topic, and my enthusiasm will make the reader like it.
- I thought of the needs and interests of my audience throughout the paper.
- The voice of this piece is perfect for my purpose.

5
- This voice stands out from others. It's personal.
- The reader might want to share this paper aloud—I would.
- I like this topic, so a lot of energy comes through.
- I considered my audience, and I think this voice is right.
- The voice is just right for my purpose.

4
- My voice comes through clearly in parts.
- The reader might share moments here and there.
- I like this topic for the most part. The writing has some energy.
- I think the voice is an OK match for my audience.
- My voice seems OK for my purpose.

3
- I am not sure if this paper sounds like me or not.
- This paper isn't quite ready to share aloud yet.
- I could not get too excited about this topic.
- I was writing to get done, not writing for an audience.
- I do not know if this voice fits my purpose.

2
- I do not think this sounds much like me.
- This paper is NOT ready to share aloud. There isn't enough voice!
- I did not like this topic. I think I sound a little bored or tired.
- I just wanted it to be over. I don't care if anyone reads this.
- Since I am not sure what my purpose is, I don't know if my voice fits or not.

1
- I do not hear any voice in this writing.
- Share this aloud? Not for anything!
- This topic was so-o-o-o boring—plus I didn't know much about it!
- Why would anyone want to read this? I don't even like it myself.
- I do not know what my purpose for writing this is.

Recommended Books for Teaching Voice

Read as you'd like to hear your students read—with expression and energy! Ask students questions like these: *How would you describe the Voice? What strategies does this writer use to put voice into his or her writing?*

Chipman, Dawn, Mari Florence, and Naomi Wax. 2001. *Cool Women: The Thinking Girl's Guide to the Coolest Women in History.* Chicago: 17th Street Press. A mix of voices from multiple authors enriches the history and sense of perspective.

Courtney, Bryce. 1989. *The Power of One.* New York: Ballantine Books. A powerful central voice by the unique voices of other characters.

Feiffer, Jules. 2002. *By the Side of the Road.* New York: Hyperion. Imaginative and filled with voice. Excellent dialogue.

Flake, Sharon G. 2000. *The Skin I'm In.* New York: Hyperion. The story of Maleeka Madison, told in her own highly individual, unflinchingly honest voice.

Korman, Gordon. 2000. *No More Dead Dogs.* New York: Hyperion Books for Children. Hysterically funny story of Wallace Wallace, one of the best read-aloud books in years.

McGammon, Robert R. 1991. *Boy's Life.* New York: Star Pocket Books. One of the great coming-of-age books, told in first person through the eyes of its protagonist.

Paulsen, Gary. 1977. *The Foxman.* New York: Penguin (Puffin Books). Life, love, friendship, and loss—all told in powerful, spare prose style.

Pullman, Philip. 1997. *The Subtle Knife.* New York: Del Rey Books. Lyrical, dark voice in an excellent fantasy tale. Strong female lead character.

Sebranek, Patrick, Dave Kemper, and Verne Meyer. *Write Source 2000.* 1999. Wilmington, MA: Great Source. User-friendly information on revising for voice, creating an engaging voice, creating personal writing, and many other voice-related topics.

Spinelli, Jerry. 2002. *Loser.* New York: HarperCollins Publishers. Easy reading belies profound themes of life and acceptance in this unforgettable tale.

More Ideas

Looking for more ideas on using literature to teach the trait of voice? We recommend *Books, Lessons, Ideas for Teaching the Six Traits: Writing at Middle and High School,* published by Great Source. Compiled and annotated by Vicki Spandel. For information, please phone 800-289-4490.

Lesson 9

A Defining Moment

For use with pages 41–45 in the Student Traitbook

Students who develop an "ear" for voice have a better understanding of what voice means. They develop this ear by listening to different voices and responding to them orally or through their writing. As their understanding grows, they develop a personal definition of voice that they can use in examining their own writing. In this lesson, they will make a start in developing such a definition.

Objectives

Students will respond to several different voices and use their responses to develop a personal definition of voice.

Skills Focus

- Listening for voice
- Describing different voices
- Developing a personal definition of voice

Time Frame

Allow about 40 minutes for this lesson. Devote most of the time to reading the samples aloud and discussing what students hear. Allow some time for writing and sharing reflections after students create their personal definitions of voice.

Setting Up the Lesson

Before proceeding with the lesson, use Student Traitbook page 41 to introduce or review the trait of voice.

This is a lesson about hearing and responding to a variety of voices. Think of the books you love, those you enjoy sharing aloud. Identify two or three favorite passages, and share them with students. Then invite responses. You may wish to have students bring in their own favorite passages to share aloud. If time permits, share five or six short samples and discuss the different "flavors" in which voice presents itself. For contrast, you may wish to share some relatively voiceless pieces. Examples abound: legal contracts, excerpts from some manuals, textbooks, or encyclopedias. The purpose is to get your students listening for voice and thinking about what specific features (lively words, intriguing details, enthusiastic tone) contribute to a strong voice in writing.

Teaching the Lesson

Three to Get Ready

The instructions for this portion of the lesson call for students to read Samples 1 through 3 to themselves, more than once if they wish. You may want to vary this by reading samples aloud as students listen. Practice in advance so that you can bring out as much voice as possible. Pause after each sample so that students can complete the rating scale, from 1 to 6, showing how strong they believe the voice in each passage to be. They should also use several words to describe each voice. Encourage thoughtful responses because these words will help students create definitions later. You may wish to make class lists of descriptive words for each of the three voices.

After students have had a chance to hear and respond to all three voices, invite them to identify a favorite voice and a voice that sounds most like their own. Voice 1 may be a favorite with many students, but not many are likely to identify it as the voice that sounds most like their own, with its dark, somber, ominous tone. Voice 2, by contrast, may not be the overwhelming favorite but may be the one many students identify as closest to their own. It is a pleasant, cheerful voice, though not powerful. It might be called curious, attentive, happy, or cordial. Voice 3 is likely to be the favorite of many and may also match the personal voices of some students. It is humorous, light, excited, enthusiastic, whimsical, and energetic. To conclude this lesson, ask students to rank the three voices. Most should see Sample 1 or Sample 3 as the strongest and next strongest; the precise order is a matter of personal taste. Sample 2 lacks the energy of the other two.

The Defining Moment

In this part of the lesson, students create personal definitions of the trait of voice. They should not use a dictionary, rubric, or handbook in creating these definitions. It is important that the definitions be expressed in students' own words. Remind students to look back at the three sample passages and the words they jotted down in connection with each. If you have made a class list of descriptive words, students can refer to it as well.

Share and Compare

After students have written their definitions, they can share with one or more classmates first and then with the class as a whole. Remind students to keep these definitions readily available so that they can check their work for voice as they write.

Extending the Lesson

- Ask students to hunt for a written passage (as short as one line or as long as one paragraph) that they believe has strong voice. They should come to class prepared to read their choices aloud in their response groups; they may read some to the entire class as well. If you wish, use the 6-point rating scale to score each selection for voice.
- Is the voice in the writing or in the way it's read? Find out by having a few students read Sample 2 aloud. Is it possible to make it as energetic and intriguing as the other two? Is it possible to read Sample 1 or Sample 3 and make either sound dull? Why or why not? Discuss results.
- Have students revise Sample 2. Tell them to change the wording, add detail, project more energy, or do whatever is necessary to increase the voice. Students may then read revisions aloud and discuss them as a class.

Lesson 10

Keeping Readers Connected

For use with pages 46–49 in the Student Traitbook

Although voice enhances personal writing, informational writing can also resound with voice. This voice stems from confidence and a desire to share information. This confidence derives from thorough knowledge of the topic. To achieve this kind of voice, a writer must do his or her homework, digging for the information that will make a reader want to know more. Helping that reader make personal connections with an informational topic is the core of this lesson.

Objectives

Students will recognize that a major contributor to voice in informational writing is knowledge of the topic.

Skills Focus

- Recognizing voice in informational writing
- Describing strategies to give informational writing strong voice
- Rating and ranking informational samples for voice
- Revising a flat piece of informational writing to give it audience appeal

Time Frame

Allow about 60 minutes for this lesson.

Setting Up the Lesson

As a warm-up activity, ask students to think of the writing that in their experience has the most voice. Brainstorm a list. Students are likely to suggest novels, poems, short stories, autobiographies, and so on. Now ask for samples with weak voice. Brainstorm a second list. Suggestions will probably include directions, manuals, rulebooks, and textbooks. Ask whether the authors of these informational pieces could put voice into their writing. Share aloud some samples of strong informational writing. You might take a selection from a local newspaper or a favorite journal, or you may have a favorite book in mind. If not, select a book from the Recommended Books for Teaching Voice, page 42 of this Teacher's Guide. Your illustration can be short; the point is to show students that informational writing can be as engaging as fiction.

Teaching the Lesson

Sharing an Example: *The* Endurance: *Shackleton's Legendary Antarctic Expedition*

Encourage students to read this passage in pairs. One student should read aloud as the other listens and makes notes. Suggest that students underline any passages or phrases that are particularly strong in voice. Remind them that they will be asked to respond to the passage, noting the specific strategies that author Caroline Alexander has used (or should have used) to strengthen the voice.

Thoughts and Reactions

After partners have finished reading the passage, they should identify two things the author has done to put voice into this passage. Possible responses: writing in a conversational style, using striking language ("emperor penguins solemnly approached . . . It was as if the emperors had sung the ship's dirge."), using dialogue, building suspense (Will the ship go down? Will the explorers die?), and knowing the topic well. Make a class list of the strategies students identify. Ask how many of these techniques they have tried in their own writing. Have they tried strategies not on the list? Are there additional strategies Alexander could have used to enhance voice? If so, what are they?

Reading, Rating, and Ranking

In this portion of the lesson, students first rate each of three samples on a 6-point scale and then rank them from most to least compelling. Read samples aloud if this will help students, but first, encourage them to read the samples on their own. Remind them to try to "hear" the voice of each writer as they read. Emphasize that they are to rate the writing, not the topics. Working with partners or independently, students should write the rating number on the answer blank before making their final decisions on the rankings. All three samples should *not* receive the same rating. If they do, students are not listening closely enough.

Ranking the Voices

Students should work with a partner to review their voice ratings from *Reading, Rating, and Ranking* and decide which voice is strongest and which is weakest. When students have finished, have them share results with the class as a whole.

Most students should see Sample B as the strongest. It is suspenseful and has a strong sense of immediacy and urgency that reflect the writer's knowledge of the topic. Sample A is the second strongest. The writer seems somewhat engaged and has a reasonably good grasp of the topic. Some comments reflect common knowledge ("some are long and some are short") or are stated in a rather ho-hum manner. The most voiceless of the three passages is Sample C. The writer sounds bored and offers only generalities and nonspecific language that suggests he or she may have an opinion but only minimal knowledge of the topic.

Revising to Strengthen Voice

Students should choose one of the samples they rated as weak in voice (A or C). Give them editorial license to invent details that add voice. Students might try varying the word choice, adding details, strengthening imagery, projecting enthusiasm, and using a conversational style with dialogue.

Extending the Lesson

- Read revisions aloud and list the techniques used to strengthen the passages. Ask students to indicate which techniques they found especially effective.
- Find a passage from a textbook, set of directions, government pamphlet, encyclopedia, or other source. Ask student partners to revise the text for voice. Have them share results and discuss strategies.
- Have a weakest voice contest. Invite each student to write a short paragraph (6 sentences) on a topic of his or her choice and to make it as weak as possible. Ask students to exchange these weak passages and revise them to strengthen the voice. Read before-and-after examples aloud.

Lesson 11

Thinking About Audience

For use with pages 50–53 in the Student Traitbook

The key to matching voice and audience can be summed up in one word: *expectations.* In this lesson, students are encouraged to "tune in" to their audiences, sensing their needs and probable responses in order to hit the right note (the right voice).

Objectives

Students learn to match voice with audience and to use voice as a tool in writing the same piece for two different audiences.

Skills Focus

- Analyzing the impact of voice on an audience
- Modifying a piece of writing to match the audience
- Creating two versions of the same piece of writing to meet the needs of two different audiences and analyzing the results

Time Frame

Allow about 70 minutes for this lesson, excluding any extensions. You can divide the lesson into two parts if you wish. In Part 1 (40 minutes), ask students to analyze the passage by George Orwell and complete the portion of the lesson under "Changing the Audience, Changing the Voice." In Part 2 of the lesson (30 minutes), have students create side-by-side letters under "Flexing Your Voice" and share the results.

Setting Up the Lesson

If the voice is clear enough, the audience should be simple to identify. Try this out with your students. Read several samples (preferably photocopied so that your students cannot immediately tell the source). The samples should be diverse: a passage from a textbook, an advertisement, a film review, a page from a children's book, a paragraph from a legal document, or a set of directions. Keep samples short. In each case, ask, "Who is the intended audience? How do you know?" Students should be able to tell whether the sample is directed to male or female readers or both, whether it is for younger or older readers, and whether there is a targeted audience (such as people in the market for a new car versus general readers). Although content may provide a clue as to the audience (such as small children do not purchase automobiles or diamonds), ask how the writer uses voice to reach the intended audience.

Teaching the Lesson

Sharing an Example: *Animal Farm*

Students can read the excerpt from George Orwell's *Animal Farm* silently and then write their thoughts about how Squealer shifts his voice to convince the other animals that the power-hungry pigs are actually being fair and just. (You may wish to point out the British spelling of *organization*.)

Reflecting

After students respond in writing to the Orwell passage, talk about Squealer's voice. What words did they use to describe it? Possibilities include *coaxing, understanding, sympathetic, persuasive, conniving, tricky, phony,* and *condescending.* How does Squealer use his voice? Elicit from students that Squealer adopts a tone of sympathy that he does not feel. In one sense, he uses his voice like a weapon, and it's highly effective in getting the other animals to cooperate.

Changing the Audience, Changing the Voice

Encourage students to imagine how Squealer might act and speak later when he is recounting his story to his colleagues, the other pigs. Would he make jokes, use sarcasm, or make fun of the other animals; or would he employ a serious, courteous tone, speaking highly of the animals? Use these or other questions to get students started.

Share and Compare

Give students time to share with partners; then invite volunteers to share their responses with the class. Share your version of Squealer, too. Talk about how and why Squealer's voice shifts. What does this shift in voice say about him?

Flexing Your Voice

In this portion of the lesson, students write side-by-side letters on the same topic, aimed at two different audiences. Each letter is a request for money to fund something the student has identified as personally important. Some suggestions are included in the text, but allow students to use their own ideas. Before students write, you may wish to review the expectations of different audiences. Encourage students to make notes about the kind of voice each audience might expect. Remind them to put voice into each piece but to make sure that the voice is the right voice for the audience. Point out that it is helpful to picture the person who will receive each letter.

Share and Compare

Ask student pairs to share with each other first, reminding them to avoid telling partners which letter goes to each recipient Then, invite volunteers to share with the class, again asking listeners to see whether they can match each letter to its intended audience.

Extending the Lesson

- Extend the Squealer practice by asking each student to create a journal entry that Squealer might write later that night. Then lead a discussion of students' responses.
- Have students put another character (from real life or from literature) in Squealer's place to see how the voice changes. Offer examples such as Jerry Seinfeld, Robin Williams, Tiger Woods, Laura Bush, Harriet Tubman, Maya Angelou, Brian (from *Hatchet*), or any well-known voice. Students can also choose to write in their own voices. Volunteers may read results aloud and try to identify the voices. If the voices are difficult to identify, ask students to suggest one or two words to describe each voice.
- Music has its own voice: jazz, classical, country, hip-hop, blues, rock—each has its own unique sound. Invite students to bring in favorite music (bring your favorites, too), but go for a range of sounds. Ask these questions: "To what sort of audience does each musical 'voice' appeal, and how do you know? Could the audience sometimes surprise you?" (In other words, do we link music to only one audience when it may appeal to another group as well?)
- Ask students to review samples of their own writing and to identify the probable audience. What if there is none? What sort of revision is needed for such a piece? Have students revise to sharpen the appeal to a particular audience.

Lesson 12

Kick It into High Gear!

For use with pages 54–57 in the Student Traitbook

Voiceless writing is tired writing. A writer gets worn out, bored, indifferent—or just a bit lazy—and simply doesn't pump enough energy ("fuel") into the writing. The reader senses this and becomes just as worn out, bored, and indifferent as the writer. In this lesson, students sharpen their skills in separating high- and low-energy writing and gain practice in revising to give a tired piece a power injection.

Objectives

Students will analyze a sample of writing to identify the strategies used to achieve strong voice and then apply these techniques in revising a sample of flat writing.

Skills Focus

- Responding to writing by identifying images and feelings
- Analyzing a professional writing sample to determine what strategies are used to achieve strong voice
- Applying those same strategies to revise writing for voice

Time Frame

Allow about 55 minutes for this lesson, excluding any extensions. You can divide the lesson into two parts. In Part 1 (30 minutes), take students through the sections called "Sharing an Example: *Meely LaBauve,*" "Messin' with the Voice," "Seeing and Feeling the Difference," and "Where's the Fuel Coming From?" Discuss responses in each case. In Part 2 (25 minutes), invite students to revise the paragraph entitled "Pro Football Camp."

Setting Up the Lesson

Ask each student to jot down some thoughts about what makes him or her an individual—likes or dislikes, ways of walking or speaking, personal reflections, attitudes, and preferences. Referring to their lists, students should then think about the ways in which these individual characteristics—indicators of personal voice—emerge in their writing.

If you have the poem "Theme for English B" by Langston Hughes (this can be found on page 11 of the *Daybook of Critical Reading and Writing,* Grade 8), use it as an example of how this professional writer recounts the characteristics, thoughts, and feelings that make him who he is.

Teaching the Lesson

Sharing an Example: *Meely LaBauve*
As students read this passage, invite them to interact with the text, marking passages or words where the voice seems strong. Doing this will help them later in describing the voice. It may be helpful to read the passage aloud so that students can hear the voice more clearly.

Messin' with the Voice
Students should listen once more as you read the revised version of *Meely LaBauve.* Tell them to mark those words or phrases that seem vague, flat, or routine. What happened to the spirit, the voice of the original? Encourage discussion with prompts like these: *Which sample sounds more like the way you usually write? Is your writing bold and individual, or is it flat and nondescript?*

Seeing and Hearing the Difference
In this part of the lesson, students compare the two samples more analytically, noting specifically the images and feelings each provokes: What do they *see*? What do they *hear*? Allow time for students to complete their responses individually. Then they can compare responses with partners or share them with the class. Share your own responses as well.

Where's the "Fuel" Coming From?
Most students should agree that Sample 1 (Wells's original) has more voice and that it prompts sharper images and stronger feelings. The question is *How does Wells do it?* Ask students to list their ideas and then share with a partner. When they have finished, you may wish to compile a class list of strategies for students to use later in revising a weak sample. Here are some strategies students may notice:

1. Meely's dialect—her own highly individual way of speaking
2. Honesty—Meely is truthful and open in her observations
3. The conversational tone of the piece—Meely seems to speak directly to the reader

4. Original phrasing—*you could eat ground-up mule;* choupique *are like dinosaurs; Curious bird he is, walkin' slow as winter.*

Shifting into High Gear

This time, students will do more than analyze; they will use some of the strategies they have identified to improve the voice in "Pro Football Camp." Their revisions need not be long or complicated, but the voice should be original, confident, and engaging. Tell students not to worry if their personal knowledge of football is limited. (Students who understand the game will have a slight edge because knowledge does contribute to voice.) Emphasize that students should work with what they know. Here is a possible revision:

I thought I hated football, but that was before my grandparents took me to a Seattle Seahawks' practice near their home in Chattaroy, Washington. It was a sweltering day, and the players could run and throw only for short periods before their legs and lungs gave out and they collapsed in a heap of shoulder pads and crashing helmets. Veterans and rookies alike drank gallons of water, laughing and splashing one another.

Fans who had gathered to watch the practice cheered on their favorites with shouts of "Way to take him down!" and "Defense!" They teased the rookies mercilessly, but the new players just waved their fists in the air. Twice the ball came so close that I thought for sure I could catch it, but out of nowhere someone would spring for it and grab it from the air.

After practice the players walked so close to us that you could see the shiny sweat on their faces. They were huge and powerful, like upright lions, but they were friendly enough to stop and talk to us. One wrote "Future Star" on the brim of my hat. That's a moment I'll never forget. Hey—I'm a fan for life.

Extending the Lesson

- Make a list of strategies students used to improve voice in "Pro Football Camp." How well did their techniques work? Read some samples aloud and compare different approaches with the class. Did anyone change the title?
- Invite students to select any piece that is strong in voice and then "revise" it as we did with the excerpt from *Meely LaBauve.* When students have completed their revisions, ask volunteers to share their strategies for minimizing voice.
- Invite each student to check his or her own writing folder for a piece that needs work in voice. Students should read through the text, identify the purpose and audience, and then apply the strategies from this lesson to make the voice powerful.

Voice

Teacher's Guide pages 41, 144–155
Transparency numbers 9–12

Objective

Students will review and apply what they have learned about the trait of voice.

Reviewing Voice

Review with students what they have learned about the trait of voice. Ask students to discuss what voice means and to explain why voice is important in a piece of writing. Then ask them to recall the main points about voice that are discussed in Unit 3. Students' responses should include the following points:

- Use voice to keep readers "connected" to an informational topic.
- Match voice to audience.
- Revise to inject energy into flat, voiceless writing.

Applying Voice

To help students apply what they have learned about the trait of voice, distribute copies of the Student Rubric for Voice on page 41 of this Teacher's Guide. Students will use the rubric to score one or more of the sample papers that begin on page 116. The papers for voice are also on overhead transparencies 9–12.

Before students score the papers, explain that a rubric is a grading system that determines the score a piece of writing should receive for a particular trait. Preview the Student Rubric for Voice, pointing out that a paper very strong in voice receives a score of 6 and a paper very weak in voice receives a score of 1. Tell students to read the rubric and then read the paper they will score. Then tell them to look at the paper and the rubric together to determine the score the paper should receive. Encourage students to make notes on each paper to help them score it. For example, they might put a check mark next to a sentence in which a strong voice emerges.

Overview

This unit focuses on *Word Choice*—helping student writers think carefully about which words *speak* to a reader. Some writers (and speakers) always seem to find the right word for the audience, occasion, and message. Good writers search for the right word or phrase and perhaps try out several before settling on the best fit. Good writers use precise language to help readers connect with the text. Good writers are also eager to stretch, to find an original way to express their ideas.

The focus of instruction in this unit will be

- Selecting the right synonym for the intended meaning
- Using sensory language to create vivid impressions
- Revising to make vague, flat language more precise and vivid
- Recognizing and eliminating clutter in writing

Word Choice: *A Definition*

Word choice is the selection of precise language to fit audience, topic, and purpose. Effective word choice is the result of simplicity, sensitivity to nuances of meaning, use of sensory detail and powerful verbs, and the variety that comes from an expanded vocabulary. In business writing, language that is crisp, direct, and reader-friendly is exactly right. A research report calls for skillful use of a specialized, technical vocabulary. Word choice also calls for restraint. Effective writing is on target every time and is never cluttered or overwritten.

The Unit at a Glance

The following lessons in the Teacher's Guide and practice exercises in the Student Traitbook will help develop understanding of the trait of word choice. The Unit Summary provides an opportunity to practice evaluating papers for word choice.

Unit Overview: Word Choice

Teacher's Guide pages 56–60

The unique features of the trait of word choice are presented along with a rubric and a list of recommended books for teaching word choice.

Lesson 13: Choosing the Right Words

Teacher's Guide pages 61–63
Student Traitbook pages 58–62

The right synonyms or antonyms can stretch a writer's vocabulary. As students discover in this lesson, even slight changes in word choice influence meaning and tone.

Lesson 14: Sensory Words

Teacher's Guide pages 64–66
Student Traitbook pages 63–66

Sensory language conveys the sights, sounds, smells, tastes, and feelings of the writer's world. In this lesson, students explore the power of sensory language.

Lesson 15: Call It as You See It

Teacher's Guide pages 67–69
Student Traitbook pages 67–70

Vague words leave readers to wonder what the writer actually experienced. In this lesson, students gain practice transforming nonspecific language into a precise message.

Lesson 16: The Right Team for the Job

Teacher's Guide pages 70–72
Student Traitbook pages 71–74

In an effort to use *every* exciting, appealing word or phrase possible, some writers go too far. In this lesson, students learn that precise word choice depends more on quality than quantity. They must cut the clutter.

Unit Summary: Word Choice

Teacher's Guide page 73
Overhead numbers 13–16

Use the student rubric on page 59 and the activities in the Summary to practice evaluating writing for the trait of word choice. Remember, 5-point rubrics, along with rationales for scores on sample papers, appear in the Appendix of this Teacher's Guide, pages 192–214.

Teacher Rubric for Word Choice

6
- The writing is clear, striking, original, and precise.
- The writer understands shades of meaning and uses words appropriately.
- The writing is concise; each word counts.

5
- The writing is clear and often original. Words are generally used accurately.
- The writer understands shades of meaning and usually uses words appropriately.
- The writing is reasonably concise; a word or phrase here and there could be cut.

4
- The writing is clear in most cases. A few words or phrases are vague, confusing, or inaccurate.
- The writer generally understands shades of meaning and uses most words appropriately.
- Some writing is concise; wordy moments may crop up also.

3
- The writing is often unclear, misleading, or vague, though the main idea comes through.
- The writer doesn't fully understand shades of meaning and often misuses words.
- The writing may be short but is not necessarily concise. Some clutter is evident.

2
- Many words and phrases are misused, vague, or unclear. The reader must guess at the writer's main message.
- The writer has only beginning knowledge of shades of meaning and sometimes misuses words.
- Word use may be skeletal *or* cluttered; either way, meaning is hard to determine.

1
- Words and phrases are consistently vague, confusing, or misused.
- The writer doesn't understand shades of meaning and misuses words.
- Word choice seems random. Words create no clear meaning.

Student Rubric for Word Choice

6
- Every word contributes to the main message.
- I selected words with just the right shade of meaning.
- I got rid of clutter. Every word counts.

5
- Most of my words and phrases are clear.
- I used words that have the right meaning for my message.
- I got rid of most clutter. I don't think it's a problem.

4
- My words are usually clear. The reader can figure out my main idea.
- A few words should be replaced with more precise synonyms.
- My writing has some clutter. I could cut some words or phrases.

3
- My word choice is unclear in many places. The reader *might* guess my main idea.
- Some of my words should be replaced with more precise words.
- My writing is cluttered. I used too many words I did not need, or else my descriptions are too sketchy.

2
- My words are *very* unclear. I did not always know the meaning myself.
- Many words should be replaced with more precise words.
- I do not know for sure whether I used too many words or not enough words. I just wrote.

1
- My words are hard to understand. They are vague—or I just guessed which word to use.
- My message is unclear because I have used words inappropriately.
- Maybe I used too many words. I don't know.

Recommended Books for Teaching Word Choice

As you read aloud, pay particular attention to strong verbs, colorful words, precise phrasing, and sensory detail. Ask students questions like these: *Do you notice any effective samples of sensory language? Is the language precise? Does the writing seem wordy? Does this writer use words in an original way?*

Ambrose, Stephen E. 2001. *The Good Fight: How World War II Was Won.* New York: Atheneum. Lively, energetic nonfiction, filled with captivating illustrations.

Deuker, Carl. 1997. *Painting the Black.* New York: Avon. One friend must choose between his baseball team and doing the right thing.

Masson, Jeffrey Moussaieff. 1995. "A Capacity for Joy." In *When Elephants Weep.* New York: Bantam Doubleday Dell. Well-crafted prose highlights this intriguing nonfiction essay on how animals, like humans, experience joy in many ways.

Maxwell, Jessica. 1997. "At Home in the Whole Wide World." In *Femme d'Adventure: Travel Tales from Inner Montana to Outer Mongolia.* Seattle, WA: Adventura (Seal Press). Extraordinarily descriptive language; masterful use of verbs.

Quammen, David. 1998. "To Live and Die in L.A." In *Wild Thoughts from Wild Places.* New York: Scribner. Powerful, punchy prose in a well-researched nonfiction essay about the relentless hunting of coyotes and their incredible ability to adapt against all odds.

Rawls, Wilson. 1999. *Summer of the Monkeys.* New York: Bantam Doubleday Dell. Charming, voice-filled story set in the Cherokee Ozarks. Told in elegant, original prose. Strong verbs are evident in this perennial favorite.

Reef, Catherine. 2002. *This Our Dark Country.* New York: Clarion. Vivid, nonfiction history of the settling of Liberia (liberty), a controversial homesite established in 1822 for free blacks and former slaves.

Richardson, Bill. 2000. *After Hamelin.* Toronto: Annick Press. Rich, compelling language in a fantasy continuation of the Pied Piper story.

Severance, John B. 2002. *Braving the Fire.* New York: Houghton Mifflin. Vivid language depicts details of a soldier's everyday life and of actual battles, clearly showing the bleak side of war. Historically researched.

Tsukiyama, Gail. 1994. *The Samurai's Garden.* New York: St. Martin's. Hauntingly beautiful, elegant prose highlights this first-person story.

Lesson 13

Choosing the Right Words

For use with pages 58–62 in the Student Traitbook

Proper use of synonyms is a helpful way for students to stretch their vocabulary. Synonyms add variety and nuances of meaning to text that might otherwise be vague and repetitive. This lesson encourages students to explore the use of synonyms and antonyms and consider how to choose the right word to convey the intended meaning.

Objectives

Students will understand the nature of synonyms and antonyms and gain skill in selecting the most precise word for the job.

Skills Focus

- Understanding the nature of synonyms and antonyms
- Locating synonyms for a given word
- Distinguishing among synonyms by identifying nuances of meaning
- Recognizing the ways in which various synonyms and antonyms affect meaning and tone

Time Frame

Allow about 60 minutes for this lesson.

Setting Up the Lesson

Make sure that students understand the concept of the trait of word choice. Use page 58 in the Student Traitbook to review or introduce the concept.

Tell students that although synonyms mean approximately the same thing, they often have quite different connotations. Synonyms for *walk,* for example, might include *amble, stroll, swagger, strut, stride, creep, march, shuffle, hike, prance,* and *lurch.* Distribute 3″ × 5″ cards on which you have printed the words, and allow students to mime them for the class; then see whether observers can identify a word by the way it's "performed." Talk about slight differences in meaning and the mood each connotation creates. If you read that someone is "stumbling" down the road, what do you picture and feel? What if the person is "lurching"? Talk about how changing even one word can alter not only literal meaning but tone and mood as well.

Teaching the Lesson

Sharing an Example: *The Hostile Hospital*

Ask students to read the example, thinking particularly about the meaning of the word *spurious.* They should not share their reflections or look up the word yet. However, they may make notes or underline clues that show what the word could mean.

Reflect

In this part of the lesson, students learn that parts of speech are important in locating synonyms. Make sure everyone can identify *nouns, verbs, adjectives,* and *adverbs.* Invite students to look in a thesaurus for these distinctions. Make sure that each student knows how the part of speech is indicated in the source he or she is using. Then, ask students to identify four or more synonyms for the adjective *spurious.* They should list their synonyms and be prepared to explain differences in meaning among the terms *false, fake, counterfeit, bogus, nongenuine, feigned, deceitful, contrived, artificial, forged,* and *phony.* Students are also asked to identify one synonym that would be a good substitute for *spurious* as the word is used in *The Hostile Hospital.* Some possibilities are *fake, bogus,* and *contrived.* Disguises can look *fake;* however, they would not look *forged.*

The Right Color

This portion of the lesson focuses on levels of intensity. Here students can increase their awareness of how words affect readers. Most students should see *"He was **annoyed**"* as a low-intensity response. *Annoyed* is a mild word; synonyms are *bothered, disturbed, disgruntled. "He was **angry**"* implies that he was more than bothered; he felt genuine, red-faced anger. *"He was **furious**"* is the most intense of the three. Antonyms of matching intensity might include these:

- Low intensity: *undisturbed, indifferent, relaxed, mellow*
- Medium intensity: *happy, excited, pleased, delighted*
- High intensity: *thrilled, elated, ecstatic, jubilant*

As students share, they should compare the words they selected and how they rated intensity levels.

Extending Your Practice: More Choices

In this section, students must identify the part of speech for each word in colored print and then find three synonyms for the word. Encourage them to use a thesaurus or dictionary to support the search. Following are a few possible synonyms for each word.

- **enormous:** *huge, gigantic, gargantuan, vast, mammoth, large*
- **purchased:** *bought, acquired, obtained, got, secured, came by*
- **guardian:** *protector, defender, champion, parent, overseer, custodian*
- **putting on:** *donning, getting dressed in, changing into, slipping into*

Matching Shades

In this portion of the lesson, students are asked to identify those synonyms that come closest to matching the meaning of the author's originals. Then each student will write a new paragraph, using those synonyms. The purpose is to encourage students to think carefully about slight differences in meaning and to choose words that will not significantly alter the meaning of the original. Read responses aloud, and encourage students to comment on whether original meanings are greatly altered by any of the substitutions.

Playing with Opposites

Here, students use antonyms for identified words and so change the meaning of the passage. The purpose, again, is to show how word choice influences meaning. Antonym modification should completely change the meaning and mood of the writer's original text.

Extending the Lesson

- Brainstorm a list of "tired" words, such as *great, nice, fun, good, bad,* and *special.* Then make a list of strong synonyms for each word. Ask students to search their own recent writings for samples of these words and to replace each with a synonym that fits. Invite volunteers to read their results aloud and compare them to the originals.
- Are there some words for which no good synonyms exist? Make a class collection of such words. Then, talk about why some words have many synonyms, but others have few or none at all.

Lesson 14

Sensory Words

For use with pages 63–66 in the Student Traitbook

Sensory words allow the reader to explore the sights, sounds, smells, and feelings of the writer's world. This puts the reader "right at the scene" and helps him or her expand meaning and response through personal associations. Sensory language may not be essential to every piece of writing, but when used strategically, it can enhance any piece for which description, personal response, or setting is important.

Objectives

Students will refine their understanding of sensory language and will explore ways of using sensory language to enrich text.

Skills Focus

- Understanding the nature of sensory detail
- Identifying sensory detail in writing samples
- Using sensory detail to create original writing

Time Frame

Allow about 30 minutes for this lesson. The lesson can be divided into two parts. In Part 1 (20 minutes), ask students to read and respond to the samples from *The Fellowship of the Ring* and *A Step from Heaven.* They should complete the charts for both pieces. In Part 2 (30 minutes), each student should complete the graphic organizer under "Your Turn to Extend the Invitation" and write a short paragraph or poem based on this prewriting activity.

Setting Up the Lesson

To show students how sensory detail works, start with a sketchy version of an event: *I was walking near the pond.* Then invite them to ask questions that will encourage you to fill in details: Where are you? What can you see? Do you notice any smells in the air? Are you eating or drinking? What kind of day is it—hot, cold, rainy, snowy? Are you on a path or walking through a field? Who or what is around you? How big is the pond?

Then, "fill in the blanks." As you do so, call students' attention to the sensory details you are using: I was walking quietly on the dirt path, sipping hot chocolate, near the huge expanse of wetlands where the Canada geese gather. It was a cloudy day in late fall, and it felt like snow might be on the way. Aspen leaves were bright yellow, even on this dark day. I felt snug in my blue hooded jacket and was smiling inside, even though my cold, red face was too stiff with cold to show it. I could smell wood smoke from a nearby fire and someone cooking salmon for a late-season barbecue. Across the meadow, two coyotes were playing tag, probably scaring all the field mice out of the long, flattened yellow grass. The coyotes' shrill voices cut the cold air.

Teaching the Lesson

Sharing an Example:
The Fellowship of the Ring

Ask students to read the excerpt from *The Fellowship of the Ring* and to underline strong examples of sensory detail.

Sensory Reaction

For this part of the lesson, students should fill out the horizontal chart that has been started for them, using the underlined details they noticed. Most should have little difficulty finding at least one or two additional details for each portion of the chart. Allow students to refer to the passage and to compare notes with a partner. **NOTE:** Some details, such as the wood smoke and the fire, can fit into more than one category. You can see, hear, smell, and feel (the heat of) a fire.

Working from Scratch

Students will read the sample from An Na's *A Step from Heaven,* underline sensory words and phrases, and then fill in the chart, just as they did for *The Fellowship of the Ring.* Again, they should have no difficulty finding two or three examples for each portion of the chart. Remind students that some details may fit in more than one place. You may wish to discuss as a class how the details in the two excerpts help put readers at the scene. This is the value of description.

Your Turn to Extend the Invitation
In this part of the lesson, each student will fill in the chart as a prewriting activity and then create an original paragraph or poem, using the chart as a reference. Point out that for this part of the lesson, students will need to think of the details first and then write. Suggest that it may be helpful to put themselves in a real place. Doing so can make it easier to recall sensory details because memory and association are working for them.

Extending the Lesson

- Allow time for students to share their poems or paragraphs from the final writing practice. Comment on sensory details that are especially vivid.
- After a few days, have students revise their sensory paragraphs and poems, referring to the charts of sensory details as they work. When students have finished their revisions, ask them to explain why they added or cut details.
- Talk about how sensory details affect mood. For example, can smells create a dark, somber mood? A cheery, bright mood? Ask students to explain their responses.
- Use brief excerpts from various paragraphs and poems to create a class poem—a collage of sensations. The words and phrases may be based on different experiences or different places. Ask each student to contribute one detail. List these. The result is a "collage" poem, mixing voices and impressions from many experiences. You can read the poem aloud or ask students to do a choral reading.
- Sensory detail is an important part of advertising. Create some advertisements based on photographs of real estate, vacation spots, automobiles, sports equipment, food, restaurants, and so on. Ask student teams to work as advertising professionals, using sensory detail to entice clients. Have students read the ads aloud and post them, or help them create a class magazine.

Lesson 15 Call It as You See It

For use with pages 67–70 in the Student Traitbook

Writers who rely on vague language—often the first words that come to mind—require readers to do the hard work, coming up with specifics, images, and details. This lesson encourages students to take responsibility for clear writing, replacing vague, general words and phrases with language that is vivid, accurate, and memorable.

Objectives

Students will identify samples of vivid writing and use this knowledge to revise vague writing for word choice.

Skills Focus

- Identifying samples of vivid, energetic word choice
- Revising vague writing to make it more specific and detailed
- Creating an original piece of writing that incorporates precise language

Time Frame

Allow about 55 minutes for this lesson, excluding any extensions. In Part 1 (30 minutes), ask students to complete "Sharing an Example" and to identify striking words or phrases from each of the two excerpts. Then ask them to revise the two practice sentences in the section called "Flat to Vivid" and discuss the results with a partner. In Part 2 (25 minutes), have each student write an original short story or description under "Energetic Writing of Your Own." Allow time for student partners to share their results.

Setting Up the Lesson

Vague language annoys readers and can create any number of misunderstandings. To make this point, put students in small groups, and provide each group with a piece of text in which precise language counts: a paragraph from a history book, a newspaper account of a robbery, results of a ball game, and so on. Make sure each group has a different piece. Ask group members to "revise" their excerpts, replacing the specifics with weak, vague wording: *nice, OK, good, great, stuff, something, whatever, pretty much, kind of,* and so on. Ask a representative from each group to read that group's "revision" aloud to see whether other groups can tell what the original was about—or even what sort of writing it was supposed to be. Discuss with the class how imprecise writing affects the audience.

Teaching the Lesson

Sharing an Example: *Zack* and *The Hungry Ocean*

Invite students to read the excerpts at least twice, underlining strong, vivid words and phrases as they go. Both samples are clear and rich with detail; students should note many words and phrases.

Share and Compare

Allow time for students to share with partners. Then discuss favorite words or phrases with the class as a whole. Did many students select the same passages? Why would that happen? Would anyone change any words or phrases?

Flat to Vivid

In this portion of the lesson, students practice their revision skills on two short sentences. This practice is a warm-up for a longer writing task that will follow. The goal is to make each revision as vivid and precise as possible. There are no *wrong* answers, but the more vague language a reviser can eliminate, the better. Possible responses are these:

1. I cannot help craving the pickled mushrooms at Nibbles, my favorite restaurant in town—and I often wake up at 3 A.M. thinking about them.
2. When it's raining too hard to see across the street, my friends and I meet at the roller rink, where the

deafening rock music and the excitement of racing one another make us forget about weather.

Share and Compare

When students have shared with partners, make sure they rate themselves on the short checklist provided. Ask volunteers to share their results. Suggest that students who think they could have done better try again. Remind them that revision is an ongoing process.

Energetic Writing of Your Own

This portion of the lesson allows students to do some original writing, incorporating the most precise, striking language possible. Their first task is to choose a format: story or description. The ideas provided in the Traitbook are suggestions, and students may write on other topics if they wish. **Tip:** Suggest that students prewrite for a few minutes, as indicated in the Student Traitbook. Students may use any device they find helpful: list, sketch, word web, T-table, and so on. Point out that students may write poetry or prose.

Share and Compare

As they share their work aloud, partners should listen carefully for any vague wording and for examples of especially effective language. Remind partners to be explicit, but not overly critical, in providing feedback.

Extending the Lesson

- Invite volunteers to read their work aloud. Comment on those words or phrases that work especially well.
- Have students rewrite one or both of the book excerpts as unrhymed poems. Read some of these aloud. As a class, discuss the power of poetry to help writers focus on striking imagery and strong words. Ask students to explain why poetry can do this.
- Have students rewrite one of the book excerpts in vague, colorless language. Share the results. Ask students whether specific language can do more than provide literal meaning.
- Review random samples from newspapers, textbooks, junk mail, advertisements, and so on. (Ask each student to contribute one or two items for your class collection.) Have students classify the items. Are they colorful and specific, or vague and elusive? Some of each? Have students work together to make a continuum display. Tell students to select and cut out sample words and phrases (both strong and weak). Post them along the continuum, and rate them from vague to gaining focus to precise and vivid.

Lesson 16
The Right Team for the Job

For use with pages 71–74 in the Student Traitbook

To some writers, every word sounds so good, so meaningful, and so memorable that they can't bring themselves to delete anything. The result is clutter: a barrage of verbiage instead of a few well-chosen words. This lesson is about controlling clutter by using *only* precise and necessary words and cutting all the rest.

Objectives

Students learn to recognize clutter in writing and practice revising to make writing concise and clear.

Skills Focus

- Identifying clutter in writing
- Reviewing a wordy sample and deleting clutter
- Reviewing a wordy sample to eliminate clutter and rewriting to create a smooth, readable piece

Time Frame

Allow about 55 minutes for this lesson, excluding any extensions. You can divide the lesson into two parts. In Part 1 (30 minutes), ask students to review the passage about football camp under "Sharing an Example," indicate their response under "Reaction," and then work with a partner to eliminate the clutter. In Part 2 (25 minutes), ask students to complete the section called "Eliminating Clutter," deleting unnecessary and imprecise words, rewriting the passage, and sharing the revised version with a partner.

Setting Up the Lesson

To demonstrate cutting clutter, place a sample piece of wordy writing on an overhead. You can create your own sample or use the following: *This morning, right before afternoon, but not too early, like around 11, I thought to myself that I might go for a walk or kind of a stroll sort of in the direction of the park. I also considered how much fun it might be if I decided to take my dog along, and so I called him in from the backyard and put on his leash and off we went to the park, just the two of us, walking along, together, toward the park.*

First, do some "timid revising," cutting only a word or two. Then ask students for their advice. What should you cut? Emphasize the emergence of clear, concise writing as you incorporate their suggestions and use revision strategies of your own.

Teaching the Lesson

Sharing an Example

Students can read the excerpt on football camp silently, noting examples of wordy language as they go. Remind them to find the main idea despite the clutter, if possible.

Reaction

Discuss with students their reactions to the piece, and ask them to rate it on the checklist provided. (Most should say "Clutter with a capital *C!*") Then, before they read the revision from the Student Traitbook, ask student pairs to go through the sample again and cross out words, phrases, or whole sentences that get in the way of the message.

A Little Comparison

Students should compare their revisions to the one in the Student Traitbook, but they should not try to match their revisions to those in the text. Emphasize that there is no right answer to revision; each person's view of the text will be slightly different. The idea is to determine whether students will recognize and make major changes.

Share and Compare

Each student should complete the short checklist in light of the comparison of his or her revision with the one provided. Although an exact match is unnecessary, students who have not cut the original text by at least one-third should review their work and delete more clutter.

Eliminating Clutter

This portion of the lesson is another opportunity for students to eliminate wordiness. They will probably enjoy revising this obviously wordy and repetitive piece about monitoring a younger brother who has "rediscovered" the joys of bike riding. Encourage them to take charge of the writing, retaining only what is needed to convey the message in a clear, smooth flow of words. **HINT:** Remind students that they may reword sentences to create smooth and coherent paragraphs. A suggested revision is below. Remember, students' revisions need not match the example.

About a week ago, my younger brother "rediscovered" his bicycle. Suddenly, he's become obsessed with riding up and down in front of our house. He's a maniac. The worst part is that my parents think he needs a guardian, but as you can imagine, I have other things to do besides monitor Mr. Tour de Neighborhood. I've put everything on hold—phone, friends, games, reading—to serve as biking boy's private highway patrol. I may have to sabotage his bike to get my life back.

Extending the Lesson

- Invite students to look through their writing folders for samples that they can revise to eliminate clutter. When students have revised their work, invite them to share before and after samples in response groups.
- Create some deliberately wordy writing. Begin by asking each student to write the "core" message in a paragraph of four to six sentences. The topic is optional. Then ask students to double the length of their paragraphs without adding any significant information. Tell them to exchange paragraphs and revise to eliminate wordiness. What strategies did students "convert" to make paragraphs purposely wordy? Do writers sometimes do these things unconsciously?
- Ask students to rewrite a well-known piece of writing, such as "Happy Birthday to You" or a nursery rhyme, clogging it with clutter. What are the results? (The same activity will work with a set of simple directions, a recipe, a weather forecast, or a greeting card.)
- Point out that when people clean their attics or basements, they sometimes throw away things they later wish they'd kept. Discuss this with the class: Could this happen when you're revising? Could you cut too much? How do you know when to stop? What if you were to revise the little brother and his bike piece this way: *My little brother "rediscovered" his bike and now he can't stop riding! I have to watch him, and it's making me crazy.* To stimulate participation, ask questions like these: Has the piece been cut too much? Is it better than our first revision? Explain.

Word Choice

Teacher's Guide pages 59, 156–167
Transparency numbers 13–16

Objective

Students will review and apply what they have learned about the trait of word choice.

Reviewing Word Choice

Review with students what they have learned about the trait of word choice. Ask students to discuss what word choice means and to explain why word choice is important in a piece of writing. Then ask them to recall the main points about word choice that are discussed in Unit 4. Students' responses should include the following points:

- Select the right synonym to create the precise meaning intended.
- Use sensory language to create vivid impressions for the reader.
- Revise to make vague, flat language more precise and vivid.
- Revise to eliminate clutter.

Applying Word Choice

To help students apply what they have learned about the trait of word choice, distribute copies of the Student Rubric for Word Choice on page 59 of this Teacher's Guide. Students will use the rubric to score one or more of the sample papers that begin on page 116. The papers for word choice are also on overhead transparencies 13–16.

Before students score the papers, explain that a rubric is a grading system that determines the score a piece of writing should receive for a particular trait. Preview the Student Rubric for Word Choice, pointing out that a paper very strong in word choice receives a score of 6 and a paper very weak in word choice receives a score of 1. Tell students to read the rubric and then read the paper they will score. Then tell them to look at the paper and the rubric together to determine the score the paper should receive. Encourage students to make notes on each paper to help them score it. For example, they might circle especially strong words or draw a line through clutter.

Overview

Fluency is the grace, rhythm, and flow in writing. Thoughtful writers develop an ear for the sound and rhythm of language used well. Fluent writers read their work aloud as they write, asking, "Does this make sense? How does this sound? Do my ideas flow naturally and logically from line to line?"

The focus of instruction in this unit will be

- Listening for fluency as text is read aloud
- Distinguishing between fluent and non-fluent text
- Varying sentence beginnings to create interest
- Using transitions skillfully and sparingly
- Creating original, fluent text by applying a variety of skills

Sentence Fluency: *A Definition*

Sentence fluency is the rhythm, flow, and cadence of language. Fluency is marked by several characteristics, one of which is variety. Sentences that are varied in structure and length catch and keep the reader's attention; by contrast, repetitive sentence lengths or patterns can cause a reader to lose interest. In general, a fluent writer avoids repetition and run-ons, though either *may* appear for stylistic effect. Transitional phrases, although vital for linking ideas, must also be used with skill and restraint. Fluency and grammar are connected. For example, the fluent writer recognizes the difference between sentences and fragments but may use a fragment to emphasize a point. Oral reading is perhaps the ultimate test of fluency. Fluent writing is smooth, fluid, varied, and purposeful.

The Unit at a Glance

The following lessons in the Teacher's Guide and practice exercises in the Student Traitbook will help develop understanding of the trait of sentence fluency. The Unit Summary provides an opportunity to practice evaluating papers for sentence fluency.

Teacher Rubric for Sentence Fluency

6
- The writing is smooth, natural, and easy to read.
- Variety in sentence length and structure is striking.
- Ideas are connected logically by transitions.
- The piece invites expressive oral reading that brings out the voice.

5
- The writing is smooth and readable.
- Variety in sentence beginnings and lengths is noticeable.
- Transitions are used logically most of the time.
- The piece is a pleasure to read aloud.

4
- The writing is easy to read, despite some lapses in fluency.
- Some sentence beginnings vary; there is some variety in sentence length.
- The writer uses transitions fairly well but may occasionally overuse or omit them.
- It is easy to read this piece aloud with some rehearsal.

3
- The writing is sometimes easy to read. Choppy sentences or other problems may necessitate rereading.
- Sentence beginnings are similar; sentences tend to be the same in length.
- In many cases, the writer overuses transitions or omits them.
- Rehearsal is needed before reading this piece aloud.

2
- Choppy sentences, run-ons, or other problems slow the reader.
- The writer uses little or no variety to add interest to the text.
- Transitions are generally overused, omitted when they are necessary, or both.
- It is difficult to read this piece aloud, even with rehearsal.

1
- The writing is consistently difficult to follow or read aloud. Sentence problems abound.
- Repetition in structure is common, or it is hard to tell *where* sentences begin.
- Transitions are always overused, omitted when they are necessary, or both.
- It is very difficult to read the piece, even with rehearsal.

Student Rubric for Sentence Fluency

6
- My writing is clear, smooth, and easy to read. It flows!
- Sentences begin in many different ways. They range from short and snappy to long and smooth.
- I use transitions to connect ideas logically.
- It's easy to read this paper aloud with lots of expression.

5
- My writing is clear and smooth most of the time. It's fairly easy to read.
- I notice a lot of variety in both length and structure.
- Most of the time, I use transitions to connect ideas logically.
- The variety makes it easy to read this paper with some expression.

4
- Some of my writing is smooth. Some is choppy or repetitive.
- There is some variety in length and structure—and some repetition.
- I use transitions fairly well, but occasionally I might have overused them, omitted them where necessary, or both.
- You can make this writing sound expressive if you work at it!

3
- This writing needs smoothing out. Choppiness or repetition slows the reader.
- Many of my sentence beginnings are the same, and most of my sentences are the same length.
- I use transitions well sometimes, but too often I overuse them, forget to use them, or both.
- It is not easy to read this paper aloud, but it can be done.

2
- This writing is bumpy! The sentences do not flow.
- Too many sentences begin the same way. Too many are the same length.
- My transitions are almost always overused, omitted when they are needed, or both.
- It is hard to read this aloud. I tried, and it was hard even for me!

1
- I can't tell one sentence from another. Are these sentences?
- I'm not sure whether the beginnings are different. I'm not sure how long my sentences are!
- My transitions are overused, omitted when they are needed, or both.
- This is very hard to read aloud. I don't even want to do it myself.

Recommended Books for Teaching Sentence Fluency

Ask students questions like these when you read aloud: *Does this writer use transitions well? Are sentence beginnings and patterns varied? Does this variety contribute to fluency? Is this writing easy on the ear?*

Creech, Sharon. 2001. *Love That Dog.* New York: HarperCollins. A humorous and touching novel in free-verse style. Unique, outstanding read-aloud piece.

Dickens, Charles. 1995 (abridged edition). *A Tale of Two Cities.* New York: Puffin Penguin. History and drama combined with Dickens's unique flavor and long, graceful sentences.

Fleischman, Paul. 2000. *Big Talk: Poems for Four Voices.* Cambridge, MA: Candlewick. Excellent practice for reading aloud—can be adapted for more than four voices. Several pieces to perform.

Frank, E. R. 2002. *America.* New York: Atheneum. Gritty first-person narrative about a 15-year-old boy in a treatment center, learning to trust. Strong fluency and voice.

George, Kristine O'Connell. 2002. *Swimming Upstream: Middle School Poems.* New York: Clarion. Middle school moments captured in verse through the voice of a student new to the middle school experience.

Iqus, Toyomi. Paintings by Michele Wood. 1998. *i see the rhythm.* San Francisco: Children's Book Press. A visual and lyrical tour de force on the impact of African American music.

Lubar, David. 2002. *Dunk.* New York: Clarion Books. A snappy, compelling plot and excellent dialogue in a book that explores the nature of humor.

Pinkwater, Jill and Daniel. 2002 (new edition). *Superpuppy.* New York: Clarion. Lively personal anecdotes combine with well-written informational text.

Rappaport, Doreen. 2002. *No More! Stories and Songs of Slave Resistance.* Cambridge, MA: Candlewick. Ingenious combination of nonfiction history and narrative.

Rinaldi, Ann. 1997. *An Acquaintance with Darkness.* San Diego: Gulliver Books. Fluent, detailed historical fiction.

More Ideas

Looking for more ideas on using literature to teach the trait of sentence fluency? We recommend *Books, Lessons, Ideas for Teaching the Six Traits: Writing at Middle and High School,* published by Great Source. Compiled and annotated by Vicki Spandel. For information, please phone 800-289-4490.

Lesson 17 My Shoes... My Shoes... My Shoes...

For use with pages 75–79 in the Student Traitbook

Repetitive sentence beginnings can be dangerous for the writer who wants to get his or her message across. After all, readers absorb information best when they have not been lulled to sleep. In this lesson, students work on building variety into their writing.

Objectives

Students will gain practice in recognizing choppy writing and in revising for fluency by combining short sentences.

Skills Focus

- Listening for variety in sentence beginnings
- Experimenting with various ways to begin sentences
- Revising to increase fluency by varying sentence beginnings

Time Frame

Allow about 45 minutes for this lesson. The lesson can be divided into two parts. In Part 1 (20 minutes), students should review the example from *After Hamelin* and rate the variety in sentence beginnings. They should also underline the first few words of each sentence in "The Softball Championship Series" and read the passage aloud to a partner. In Part 2 (25 minutes), students should add variety to sentences and eliminate unneeded words in "The Softball Championship Series." Afterward, they share their revisions with partners.

Setting Up the Lesson

To introduce or review the concept of sentence fluency, use page 75 in the Student Traitbook.

This lesson focuses on the importance of varied sentence structure. Introduce your lesson by beginning every sentence with the words *Today, Yesterday,* or *Tomorrow: Today we'll be doing a lesson on fluency. Yesterday I might have mentioned something about fluency. Tomorrow we'll continue our work on fluency. Today let's have some fun writing. Tomorrow we'll review our writing.* Continue until one of your students interrupts with a comment such as "Why are you talking this way?" Ask what is unusual—or annoying—about the way you are speaking. Also, ask students if they have trouble paying attention when you talk this way. Then, discuss how a reader's mind responds to monotony in much the same way. Students should now be ready to listen for variety—or the lack of it—in sample passages.

Teaching the Lesson

Sharing an Example: *After Hamelin*
Ask students to read this passage silently, paying particular attention to the sentence beginnings in color. Most students will agree that the writing has "a great deal of variety."

Your Response
Because fluency is rated by the ear as well as by the eye, it is helpful to hear as well as see differences in sentences. Ask each of three volunteers to read one of the three paragraphs aloud as you and the rest of the class listen without reading along. Is the passage easy to listen to? (Most students should say yes.) Then, discuss the effect of variety on listeners. What if all the sentences began the same way? Would it be more difficult to listen?

Revising "The Softball Championship Series"
Before reading this text, students should underline or highlight the first three or four words of each sentence. Then, invite them to read the piece aloud to a partner and discuss it. Most students will agree that the writing lacks fluency, with most sentences beginning the same way or nearly the same way.

Beginning with Variety
Now students will revise "The Softball Championship Series" for fluency by altering sentence beginnings. Remind

the class that it is not necessary to begin EVERY sentence in a different way. Also, students may replace or add words, or change the wording or structure of sentences in order to achieve better fluency. Point out that revision is likely to require changes in punctuation. Encourage students to revise as extensively as necessary.

Share and Compare
Sharing is a vital part of any lesson on fluency. Remind students to listen for variety as their partners share. Students should help partners rate themselves on the short fluency scale: *a real improvement, some improvement,* or *not much improvement.* Those who do not hear "a real improvement" should revise again. Partners may help each other.

Extending the Lesson

- Invite volunteers to read their revisions of "The Softball Championship Series" aloud. Comment on the different strategies students used. If you like, post the students' revisions so that students can continue the comparison.
- Ask each student to review a sample of writing from his or her writing folder. Students should underline or copy (on separate paper) the first three or four words of each sentence, looking to see how much variety they can find. Then, they may revise as needed.
- How many ways are there to begin a single sentence? Ask one student to provide the rest of the class with a sample sentence. Any sentence on any topic will do. Then, ask each student to write the original sentence in as many ways as possible without changing the basic meaning. For example, *Writing can be challenging* could become *It's a challenge to write,* or *For a challenge, try writing.* Read the results aloud. The students are likely to be surprised by the many variations they can suggest.

Lesson 18 Trucking in the Transitions

For use with pages 80–83 in the Student Traitbook

The purpose of transitions—*therefore, nonetheless, however, for example*—is to show how ideas are connected, to help the reader understand the writer's thinking. Well-placed, thoughtful transitions make reading easier; too many transitions become distracting, actually clouding the writer's message. This lesson focuses on helping student writers achieve a balance.

Objectives

Students will learn to recognize transition overload and will revise an "overloaded" text so that it is easier to follow and understand.

Skills Focus

- Analyzing text that suffers from "transition overload"
- Comparing overloaded text with a well-written sample
- Revising text to eliminate the problem of transition overload

Time Frame

Allow about 60 minutes for this lesson. You can divide the lesson into two parts if you wish. In Part 1 (30 minutes), review the overloaded "revision" of the passage from *All Quiet on the Western Front* and ask students to rate it for fluency. Also ask students to read and compare the original version under "The Original." Allow time for discussion and comparison of the two passages. In Part 2 (30 minutes), invite students to read and revise the passage on firefighting. Allow time for students to share, compare, and review their results.

Setting Up the Lesson

Because this lesson focuses on the concept of overload, you might begin with a simple demonstration. Bring in a package that you are allegedly planning to mail, and ask students whether they mind your taking just a minute or two to finish taping it. Add some tape to each corner, and then go around the box, first one way and then the other. Continue taping until someone comments that you seem to have more than enough! Tell them, "You can never have too much tape," and continue working until you get more comments. Finally, tell the purpose of your demonstration, pointing out that anything can be overdone. Now introduce an "overtaped" passage.

Teaching the Lesson

Sharing an Example: *All Quiet on the Western Front*

Ask each student to work with a partner in reading this passage aloud. One partner should read the first half of the example, up to the words "To illustrate," in line seven. Students should then switch roles.

Your Reaction

Before discussing the passage with the entire class, ask partners to rate it on this short scale. When everyone has completed the rating, discuss the impact of the transition overload on a reader or listener. Most students will agree that too many transitions create confusion rather than enhance clarity.

The Original

Here is the same passage without the added transitions. You may wish to read the passage aloud so that students can focus on listening to the difference between the two versions. Then, have students complete the short checklist that follows. Most should agree that the original is easier to read and follow. Some students may note that the original is not free of transitions. Point out that transitions are helpful but that they become a problem when overused.

Too Many Transitions

Now students will take a passage from transition overload to fluency by cutting unnecessary transitions. In the next part of the lesson, they will rewrite, making additional changes.

Smoothing Things Out

Direct students to change wording, move words around, combine sentences, and alter punctuation as necessary. However, remind them to focus on eliminating transition overload, not altering the meaning of the passage. Each student should write out a revision and plan to share it aloud with a partner. **Hint:** Writers often read their own text aloud as they write to check for sound and flow. Students can do this *softly* to themselves.

Here's one suggestion for revision. Students' revisions do not need to match this one. Additions or changes in capitalization appear in boldfaced print:

~~Incredibly enough~~, **I**t's that time of year again when smoke fills the sky and ~~in addition~~ news about wildfires fills the front pages. ~~and to sum up~~, ~~dominates the local TV news. For this reason, it's no surprise to see~~ **G**roups of young men and women **are** ~~moreover, at the airport~~ heading out ~~not surprisingly~~ to join hotshot crews destined for the fires' front lines. As of yesterday, there were still seven fires burning, even though crews have been out fighting the fires for weeks. ~~Additionally~~, **H**elicopters equipped with huge buckets used to dump water on the worst spots have been seen flying back and forth ~~across the sky~~. Among those leaving the airport ~~nevertheless~~ are fire crew members ~~finally~~ returning for some badly needed rest.

Share and Compare

Ask student pairs to read their revisions aloud and to rate themselves as a team. Share results aloud, along with specific strategies the revisers used.

Extending the Lesson

- Review the original passage from *All Quiet on the Western Front.* Ask students to underline transitional words or phrases. Are there many in this original? (Yes) How does a skillful writer know when the writing has enough transitions to carry the message without obscuring it?
- Ask students to find short passages that use transitions with grace. Read a few aloud.
- Organize students in groups of four. Have each group create a short passage. Invite students to add as many transitions as possible without making their work sound ridiculous. Groups may exchange their passages and rewrite, comparing revisions to originals.
- Ask students to review samples of their own writing for transitions. Do they use enough? Too many? Just the right amount?

Lesson 19

Famous for Flow

For use with pages 84–87 in the Student Traitbook

What makes a great river like the Mississippi flow along smoothly? A solid, smooth riverbed—no obstacles; fine weather; and enough water to keep the flow going. Writing, like a river, has its own flow and pacing. When it gets diverted or has to force its way over obstacles (such as transition logjams), you can see and hear the difference. This lesson invites students to explore the specific features of writing that keep the flow of writing steady and rhythmic.

Objectives

Students will analyze samples and identify features that enhance or obstruct fluency.

Skills Focus

- Analyzing samples of writing for fluency
- Identifying specific textual features that contribute to fluency
- Ranking samples for fluency
- Revising a sample to improve fluency

Time Frame

Allow about 65 minutes for this lesson.

Setting Up the Lesson

Analysis is the focus of this lesson. Use an example outside of academics to help students understand what makes analysis work. Some possibilities include a family reunion, a film, an outing at the beach, or a first week with a new pet. Choose one of these (or your own example), and then create a T-table, listing on one side the things that make your example work well, and on the other side the things that get in the way. Tell students to copy this table or make their own. Following this discussion, let students know you will be working on identifying specific features that contribute to fluency: rhythm, sound, and effective sentence crafting.

Teaching the Lesson

Sharing an Example: *Troy*

Ask student pairs to take turns reading aloud this passage from Adele Geras' *Troy.* During the reading, students should ask themselves what elements contribute to the fluency of the passage. They should also identify any fluency problems. Tell students to mark the passage by underlining, circling, or making notes. These marks will be useful during their upcoming analyses.

After reading and marking the text, student partners should complete the list under "Elements of Fluency: How do writers create fluency?" Remind them that they may have fewer or more than six items.

Take a few minutes to share items from students' lists and to make a class list, noting those features that are mentioned most often. Possibilities (in addition to the two listed in the Student Traitbook) are *variations in sentence length, use of questions and statements, skillful repetition of some words or phrases for emphasis, use of ellipses to create a natural pause,* and *a conversational style that sounds like natural speech.* Did your students think of others? Did they identify any fluency problems?

Measuring the Flow: Read and Rank

In this part of the lesson, students should read and rank Samples A, B, and C for fluency, identifying the most fluent to least fluent passages. Partners may take turns reading each passage; that is, for each sample, each partner will listen once and read once.

Fluency Rankings

Students should rank samples individually. Comparisons will come later. Remind them to refer to their Elements of Fluency lists and to their fluency rubrics for hints on what to look for. Point out that a sure sign of fluency is readability. Students who are unsure of a passage's fluency should read it aloud.

Most students should see Sample B as the most fluent. It has variety in structure and length, and has a lively, conversational tone. Transitions are used effectively but with restraint. Next is Sample A. Despite some variety in sentence beginnings, this writer uses too many "I's." Nevertheless, the piece is easy to read (except for one overly long sentence tucked in the middle), and the sentences vary in length. Sample C is the weakest. It contains unexpected and ineffective fragments and run-ons and much repetition. It is difficult to read.

Revision Time

For this part of the lesson, students will work individually. Later, they share their revisions with partners. Each student should choose either Sample A or Sample C to revise for fluency. Students need not work on other traits, but they are likely to see improvements in voice and ideas as well as in fluency.

Students can share samples with partners first and then with the entire class. Note the specific strategies students used in their revisions.

Extending the Lesson

- Make a class list of students' revision strategies. Compare this list with the Elements of Fluency list created earlier in the lesson. Did students make use of every available strategy? Did they overlook anything?
- Read some revised samples aloud, and compare them with the originals. As an alternative, ask partners to read each other's revisions. Reading should be simple if the fluency is strong.
- Create a Fluency Scrapbook with samples of writing that you and your students collect from various sources over a four-to-six-week period. Rate the samples as strong, moderate, or weak in fluency, and keep the scrapbook handy so that students can browse through it. Samples can be marked, as long as they remain readable. Any student who contributes to the scrapbook rates the contribution.
- Punctuation is generally a part of the trait of conventions, but it contributes to fluency as well. Discuss ways in which punctuation marks affect fluency. Ask each student to each identify one short passage with a variety of punctuation marks and to rewrite it without punctuation. Have student pairs exchange papers and fill in the missing punctuation. After comparing students' versions with originals, discussion how punctuation affects fluency.

Lesson 20

Smooth Sailing

For use with pages 88–90 in the Student Traitbook

Throughout this unit, students have practiced several fluency skills: varying sentence beginnings to create interest, using transitions with restraint, and listening to text to determine specific strengths or problems. Now they will put these and other fluency-related skills together.

Objectives

Students will practice assessing and revising personal text for fluency. They will also apply what they know in a response group to help other writers improve their revisions.

Skills Focus

- Identifying text that needs revision for fluency
- Offering constructive feedback to other members of the response group
- Using personal assessment and comments offered by response group members to revise a piece of writing for fluency
- Assessing results of personal revision

Time Frame

Allow 65 minutes for this lesson. If you wish, you can divide the lesson into two parts. In Part 1 (35 minutes), each student should select a sample of personal writing from his or her writing folder to revise for fluency and complete a brief planning chart under "Charting a Course for Revision." In Part 2 (30 minutes), each student will use his or her own assessment together with the comments of the group to revise samples for fluency.

Setting Up the Lesson

This lesson has two parts: (1) sharing and responding, followed by (2) assessment and revision. Both are critical to the success of the lesson. Introduce this lesson by discussing the kinds of comments that are helpful in a response group as well as those that are not. Emphasize the need to keep comments positive but honest. Brainstorm with the students for examples of positive and negative feedback. List these in two columns, and post them where students can refer to them when analyzing one another's work. Here are some examples of things not to say:

- *That doesn't sound right.*
- *Your sentences don't work.*
- *I don't like it.*
- *The fluency isn't very good.*

Constructive comments are specific and leave the writer options. Here are some positive comments and suggestions:

- *You seem to have a lot of transitions. Do you think you need them all?*
- *It sounds to me as if a lot of sentences were about the same length—you might want to check that.*
- *I like the variety in sentence lengths.*
- *The first part of your paper has a lot of sentence variety—do you think the second part has as much?*
- *The transitions are smooth and link ideas well.*
- *A lot of sentences seem short. Could you combine some?*
- *Your writing sounds smooth, and you read with lots of expression.*

Teaching the Lesson

Captain's Choice

Give each student time to look through his or her writing folder for a sample that needs work on fluency. Students may also choose a report from another class. Remind students to look for a writing sample that specifically needs revision for fluency.

Teaming Up

Organize the class in response groups of three to five students. Review the roles of Writer and Responder as outlined in the Student Traitbook, page 89. Remind students to

- read their papers with expression.
- read without apologies—everyone recognizes that these are drafts.
- listen attentively as others read.
- offer constructive, specific, positive comments.
- make notes on teammates' comments.

Circulate among the groups, noting particularly good comments students offer. Read these aloud after groups have completed their sharing.

Charting a Course for Revision

Before students start revising, allow five minutes for them to "chart a course"—that is, make a revision plan. They can do this by completing the short checklist provided, marking each fluency problem they intend to address. In filling out the chart, students should use notes from their group sessions, along with their own judgment.

Write Now!

As students work on their revisions, encourage them to refer to their notes, checklists, and student rubrics for fluency. Remind them to read their revisions aloud before sharing.

Share and Compare

Students should read their revisions aloud to just one or two partners. Is the fluency now strong, fairly strong, or in need of further revision? Partners must be from the original response group so that they have heard the original draft. Ask students, in teams, to jot down two or three specific strategies they used to revise for fluency. They should also note any useful comments and share these with the class.

Extending the Lesson

- Continue the revision begun in this lesson. Ask students to set their writing aside for three days or more and then return to revising for fluency and other traits. Ask students to review all three drafts and to rate themselves as revisers. Are they timid (barely touched a thing)? Moderate (made one or two good changes)? Bold (made many good changes and altered the whole sound of the paper)? You may wish to have the students write journal entries in which they analyze themselves as revisers.
- Tell students to look at their revised writing for other traits. Although they were focusing on fluency specifically, did their revisions also affect word choice, ideas, voice, or any other trait? If so, how and why did this happen?
- Invite one of the response groups to model the sharing process. Group members should select samples to share and then read and comment on one another's work while the rest of the class observes. The response group of three to five students should sit in the middle of the class, with other students surrounding them. Only group members should speak during the sharing, but other students can offer feedback when the session ends. Observers should comment specifically on the readings (Did writers read with expression and without apology?) and on the quality of the comments (Which comments were especially helpful or original?).

Sentence Fluency

Teacher's Guide pages 77, 168–179
Transparency numbers 17–20

Objective

Students will review and apply what they have learned about the trait of sentence fluency.

Reviewing Sentence Fluency

Review with students what they have learned about the trait of sentence fluency. Ask students to discuss what sentence fluency means and to explain why sentence fluency is important in a piece of writing. Then ask them to recall the main points about sentence fluency that are discussed in Unit 5. Students' responses should include the following points:

- Distinguish between fluent and nonfluent text.
- Vary sentence beginnings to create interest.
- Use transitions skillfully and sparingly.
- Create original, fluent text by applying a variety of skills.

Applying Sentence Fluency

To help students apply what they have learned about the trait of sentence fluency, distribute copies of the Student Rubric for Sentence Fluency on page 77 of this Teacher's Guide. Students will use the rubric to score one or more of the sample papers that begin on page 116. The papers for sentence fluency are also on overhead transparencies 17–20.

Before students score the papers, explain that a rubric is a grading system that determines the score a piece of writing should receive for a particular trait. Preview the Student Rubric for Sentence Fluency, pointing out that a paper very strong in sentence fluency receives a score of 6 and a paper very weak in sentence fluency receives a score of 1. Tell students to read the rubric and then read the paper they will score. Then tell them to look at the paper and the rubric together to determine the score the paper should receive. Encourage students to make notes on each paper to help them score it. For example, they might underline sentence beginnings that are identical or nearly so.

Overview

As students will discover in this unit, conventions clarify and enhance the other traits. Clearly, accuracy in conventions promotes readability. A reader who does not have to edit mentally as he or she goes along can more readily focus on and appreciate a writer's thoughts and style.

The focus of instruction in this unit will be

- understanding the differences between revision and editing
- spotting errors in faulty text
- recognizing and applying sixteen editing symbols
- creating a personal editing checklist

Conventions: *A Definition*

The trait of conventions addresses spelling, punctuation, grammar and usage, capitalization, and such paragraphing indicators as indentation and spacing. Conventions may also include presentation on the page: general layout, headings and subheadings, formatting, use of fonts for stylistic effect, and incorporation of graphics. Although presentation items are not specifically addressed in this unit, it is appropriate to consider such visual conventions in assessing written work for which layout is critical. For the present, however, the focus is on evaluating text for correctness. Students need to be skilled independent editors, using conventions in ways that enhance the message and the writer's voice.

The Unit at a Glance

The following lessons in the Teacher's Guide and practice exercises in the Student Traitbook will help students develop an understanding of the trait of conventions. The Unit Summary provides an opportunity to practice evaluating papers for conventions.

Unit Introduction: Conventions

Teacher's Guide pages 92–96

The unique features of the trait of conventions are presented along with a rubric and a list of recommended resources for teaching conventions.

Lesson 21: Straighten It Up

Teacher's Guide pages 97–99
Student Traitbook pages 91–95

By reviewing examples and considering their own writing, students distinguish between revising and editing and then create personal definitions of each term.

Lesson 22: Gliding Down the Highway

Teacher's Guide pages 100–102
Student Traitbook pages 96–99

A personalized checklist helps students pinpoint errors that could impair readability in their work. With practice, they can reduce the list, one problem at a time.

Lesson 23: How Symbolic!

Teacher's Guide pages 103–106
Student Traitbook pages 100–103

In this lesson, students are introduced to sixteen editing symbols. They also practice interpreting the symbols and applying them to faulty text.

Lesson 24: The Editing Express Lane

Teacher's Guide pages 107–111
Student Traitbook pages 104–107

Practice, the key to skillful editing, is the focus of this concluding lesson. Students continue using editing symbols to mark, interpret, and correct errors from the point of view of both reader and writer.

Unit Summary: Conventions

Teacher's Guide page 112
Overhead numbers 21–24

Use the student rubric on page 95 and the activities in the Summary to practice assessing writing for the trait of conventions. Remember that 5-point rubrics, along with rationales for scores on sample papers, appear in the Appendix of this Teacher's Guide, pages 192–213.

Teacher Rubric for Conventions

6
- The text contains few or no errors. Their impact is insignificant.
- The writer uses conventions skillfully to bring out meaning and voice.
- The writer shows control over a wide range of conventions for this grade level.
- This piece is virtually ready to publish.

5
- A few errors are noticeable if the reader hunts for them. None affect clarity.
- The writer often uses conventions to enhance meaning or voice.
- The writer shows control over most conventions appropriate to this grade level.
- This piece is ready to publish after minor corrections are made.

4
- Errors are noticeable but do not impair meaning or slow a reader's pace.
- The writer uses conventions with enough skill to make the text readable.
- The writer controls grade-appropriate conventions more often than not.
- A final edit is needed before publication.

3
- Distracting errors begin to slow the reader, although the message remains relatively clear.
- Some conventions are used correctly, but serious errors affect readability.
- The writer knows some conventions but is not yet in control.
- Thorough editing is needed before publication.

2
- The number of errors makes reading a chore.
- Some conventions are used correctly, but serious errors consistently impair readability or slow the reader.
- The writer knows a few conventions but is not yet in control.
- Line-by-line editing is required before publication.

1
- Serious, frequent errors make this text hard to read, even with effort and patience.
- The reader must search to find conventions used correctly.
- This writer is not in control of most conventions appropriate for this grade level.
- Thorough, word-by-word editing is required for publication.

Student Rubric for Conventions

6
- Readers will really have to hunt to find any errors in my paper!
- I used conventions to clarify my message and to bring out the voice.
- I edited this paper thoroughly and am sure that I found and corrected all errors.
- I looked and listened for errors more than once. This paper is ready to publish.

5
- Readers may find a few errors—but they will have to hunt for them!
- My conventions help clarify my message.
- I checked my paper well, and I am sure I corrected the major errors.
- I looked and listened for mistakes. I might have missed some small errors. This paper is almost ready to publish.

4
- Readers will notice some errors. I need to edit more carefully.
- My message is still clear.
- I checked my paper quickly, but I should probably take another look.
- This paper will need careful editing before it is ready to publish.

3
- I have too many errors. This draft is still pretty rough!
- I did some things correctly, but I'm not sure that my message is always clear.
- In reviewing my paper, I see errors in spelling, punctuation, or grammar that could slow a reader's pace.
- This paper needs major editing. It is not ready to publish.

2
- I have so many errors! This paper is hard to read.
- I did a few things correctly, but mistakes interfere with my message.
- My spelling, punctuation, and grammar errors will definitely slow a reader.
- I need to read this aloud and edit it line by line before I publish it.

1
- I made so many mistakes that I can hardly read this myself.
- It is hard to find items that are done correctly or to tell what my message is.
- I see many different types of errors here.
- I need to read this aloud, work with a partner, and edit my paper word by word before I publish it.

Recommended Books for Teaching Conventions

Although we recommend the use of the student writing handbook *Write Source 2000* (see annotation below), no extended book list is included with these lessons because any reliable standard text can help you teach conventions. We encourage you to use sections from students' favorite books to talk about writers' skills in using conventions and also about how conventions help bring out meaning. Commas and semicolons indicate pauses in thought, for instance, and quotation marks indicate speech. Dashes, italics, boldface type, or ellipses are often used to influence the way a reader "hears," or interprets, a passage. As always, it is the meaning behind the convention that counts. As you share published text, be sure to notice:

- Various conventions authors have used to make meaning clear
- Authors' use of conventions to enhance voice
- Any conventions that may be new to students
- Conventions that students would change on the basis of personal style
- Any typographical errors (These are not often seen in published books, although they do appear occasionally. Such errors are quite common in newspapers, advertisements, mailings, or any publication for which the review/editing process is necessarily rapid.)

You will find many lessons, strategies, explanations, and tips to help students work successfully with conventions in the following handbook:

Sebranek, Patrick, Dave Kemper and Verne Meyer. 1999. *Write Source 2000.* Wilmington, MA: Great Source. Helpful, user-friendly information on agreement, use of modifiers, and parts of speech; correction of errors in conventions; revising and editing; use of checklists; correct usage; problem words; proofreading, punctuation, spelling; editing symbols; citations and bibliographies; and many other terms and concepts related to conventions.

More Ideas

Looking for more ideas on using literature to teach the trait of conventions? We recommend *Books, Lessons, Ideas for Teaching the Six Traits: Writing at Middle and High School,* published by Great Source. Compiled and annotated by Vicki Spandel. For information, please phone 800-289-4490.

Lesson 21

Straighten It Up

For use with pages 91–95 in the Student Traitbook

Revising and editing are related parts of the writing process, but they involve making different types of changes. Revising involves broad changes, such as adding or deleting information and re-ordering information. Editing involves attention to detail—correcting errors in spelling, punctuation, grammar, and so on—that might slow a reader down. This lesson helps students distinguish between these two important steps and develop personal definitions that will help in reworking their own and others' writing.

Objectives

Students will deepen their understanding of revising and editing, recognize samples of each process, and create personal definitions for both terms.

Skills Focus

- Reviewing samples of revised or edited text to identify changes and to distinguish between revising and editing
- Classifying specific changes as examples of either revising or editing
- Creating personal definitions for *revising* and *editing*

Time Frame

Allow about 40 minutes for this lesson.

Setting Up the Lesson

This lesson helps students understand the differences between revising and editing. Start the lesson by reviewing page 91 in the Student Traitbook. Then explain that revision involves major textual changes that evolve from a writer's continued thinking about a topic. In revising, a writer may rearrange information, add details, make more precise word choices, or delete portions of text. Editing, while equally important, involves different changes: the correction of errors in spelling, punctuation, grammar, and so on. To help students picture these differences, share a simple example: *A woman combs her windblown hair.* Is she "editing" or "revising"? We'd call this "editing" because the change is small. The hair is the same; it just looks neater. But suppose that the woman's hair is three feet long and she has it cut to just below her ears. We'd call this revising because the entire look of the hair has changed. Now use another example, and have students fill in the blanks. Start with a car: *Editing* might be—(washing the car, vacuuming the upholstery, polishing the chrome). *Revising* might be—(installing a new engine, adding a sun roof, doing major body repair). When students understand the distinction, they can apply it to writing.

Teaching the Lesson

Before and After: Notice the Difference?

Students should read the examples silently, pausing after each to jot down as many *kinds of* changes as possible. (Emphasize that these should not be specific changes, but kinds of changes, such as inserting missing words or combining sentences.) Next, students will determine whether the changes signify revising or editing. In Sample 1, the writer expands thoughts, adds detail, combines sentences, alters word choice, adds voice, and smooths out the choppiness of the original. This is clearly revision. In Sample 2, the writer corrects spelling and punctuation, eliminates repeated words, adds missing words, and changes grammar and capitalization. These corrections are examples of editing.

Share and Compare

Allow time for student partners to compare their personal analyses and talk about the kinds of changes each noticed in Samples 1 and 2. Most partners will agree on the question of whether the changes are examples of revising or editing. Discuss students' conclusions as a class.

Narrowing It Down
Students can demonstrate their understanding of revising and editing by reviewing four examples. Our answers:

1. Revising
2. Revising
3. Editing
4. Revising

Definitions
Now students can create personal definitions of *revising* and *editing.* Remind them not to use a dictionary or any other written resource to create the definitions; they should draw on their own perceptions and experience.

Extending the Lesson

- Ask students to share their definitions. They can read them aloud or post them. Be ready to share your own definitions as well.
- Invite students to review their writing and ask some reflective questions: *Does my writing need more revising or editing? A balance of both? Why?*
- Review Samples 1 and 2 and talk about the impact of revising and editing on the reader. Ask students which process makes a greater impression—or are the processes equally important, but in different ways?
- Ask students to brainstorm some personal changes that people make in their lives, such as getting a pet, changing a hairstyle, giving up junk food, or making a new friend. (You can do this brainstorming individually or as a class.) Invite students to use the results to create "Editing My Life" or "Revising My Life" poems to be shared. Write one of your own, too.
- Point out that in real-world publishing, the writer and the editor are seldom the same person. Ask students to explain why this is true. Then ask about revising—is it important that a writer do his or her own revising? Should someone else do it? Tell students to explain their answers.

Lesson 22

Gliding Down the Highway

For use with pages 96–99 in the Student Traitbook

We could provide an editing checklist for students, but using a generalized checklist is much like wearing someone else's shoes: the shoes may cover your feet, but the fit is likely to make you uncomfortable. In this lesson, students will create checklists based on the careful and honest review of their own work.

Objectives

Students will develop personalized editing checklists to help them eliminate their writing problems.

Skills Focus

- Reviewing text for editorial problems
- Prioritizing and listing personal editing problems
- Comparing and sharing lists with a partner
- Identifying an editorial problem to eliminate within the next two weeks

Time Frame

Allow about 55 minutes for this lesson. In Part 1 (20 minutes), review the student sample under "If I Were You," brainstorming the kinds of problems students observe in the text. Prioritize and refine the brainstormed list to create a sample personalized checklist appropriate to this writer's work. This checklist will be a model for students. In Part 2 (35 minutes), ask students to create individual checklists by completing the section "Make a List," comparing lists with a partner, and setting one editorial goal under "The Shrinking List."

Setting Up the Lesson

In this lesson each student will create a personal editing checklist—but it will be effective only if the student's review of his or her work is completely honest. Model such a review for the class, choosing a draft in which your writing is not editorially perfect. Distribute copies of pieces you have written or share them on the overhead. Make sure these examples contain errors that students have learned to identify. Ask students to help you brainstorm a list of the mistakes you need to address. If students seem reluctant to criticize your work, point out flaws and list them yourself. Remind students that honesty is crucial for developing an "editor's eye."

Teaching the Lesson

If I Were You

As a warm-up for designing their own lists, students will review another writer's work and compile a checklist specific to that writer's editing problems. Because the writer is anonymous, students should have no trouble being completely honest in their analyses. Student partners may work together on this activity. Ask them to prioritize by putting the problems that most demand attention at the top of the checklist. Problems students may identify include failing to capitalize the pronoun *I,* repeating words, interchanging *there* and *their,* omitting end punctuation, and misusing quotation marks. Encourage students to think of this activity as a model for reviewing their own work.

Make a List

This is the central part of the lesson. Students should review thoroughly at least two samples of their own writing, and more if time permits, because this exercise provides an accurate picture of overall editing performance. Students may review both rough and final drafts. Remind them to be honest in assessing their work. As in the previous exercise, students should prioritize, placing the most significant problems first on their lists. Students need not fill in all ten slots, but those who find fewer than four problems should analyze their work again.

Share and Compare

When students have completed their work, allow partners to share the checklists (but not the writing samples). Ask students to checkmark similarities and to note any items on a partner's list that should be added to their own. Partners may also help each other prioritize editing problems. Stress that problems most likely to hinder reader comprehension should be listed first.

The Shrinking List

Ask students to read this section silently. Then discuss the importance of using the personalized list. Make a class plan for doing so. Will students keep lists in their notebooks or portfolios? Will you post sample lists? Invite each student to identify and underline one problem on his or her list that will be the first target for change. As students do this, they should think of (1) the importance of the item to good editing and (2) their ability to overcome this editing challenge. It's best to begin with an item that can be overcome without undue frustration.

Extending the Lesson

- Invite a few students to share their review processes (they need not share their writing). They can talk about what they found, share their lists with the class, and identify those items they have targeted for immediate attention.
- Make a poster of "targeted editorial problems" for the class. Remind students to look for these particular items when helping partners and when editing their own work. Think of these items as "team targets," and see how many (as a team) students can eliminate within two weeks. Then, create a new set—keep the momentum going!
- Invite students to bring in pieces of writing that contain editorial problems. Point out that junk mail is a good source. As a class, review these samples and create personalized checklists for the writers. Performed periodically, this exercise helps students develop an "editor's eye"; it also reminds them that every editor needs a checklist.
- Discuss with students whether editing word-processed manuscript is the same as or different from editing handwritten papers. What errors are the same? What errors are different?

Lesson 23

How Symbolic!

For use with pages 100–103 in the Student Traitbook

Symbols are familiar parts of our culture. Flags, pictures, and artifacts of various kinds have symbolic meaning for us. This lesson introduces students to sixteen editing symbols, some of which may be familiar from previous editing practice or work with the trait of conventions. This lesson provides practice in "reading" and interpreting these symbols.

Objectives

Students will learn or review sixteen editing symbols and will use these symbols in editing faulty text.

Skills Focus

- Identifying sixteen editing symbols
- Learning to "read" each symbol by knowing the editorial change it indicates
- Using editing symbols to mark faulty text for correction

Time Frame

Allow about 60 minutes for this lesson, excluding any extensions. In Part 1 of the lesson (30 minutes), review the chart of editing symbols, making sure students understand what each symbol means and how it is used. Then ask students to complete the section called "Warming Up with Symbols." In Part 2 of the lesson (30 minutes), ask students to edit "Traffic Jam Destiny."

Setting Up the Lesson

Determine which editing symbols students know before they look at the editing symbols chart. (Be thoroughly familiar with the chart before you start the lesson.) Select a few symbols at random, and ask students to "read" them. What does each symbol ask the writer to do? If this exercise is too easy for your students, ask each of them to create an error for which a particular symbol would be used and exchange papers with a partner for analysis. After you have pretested students' knowledge of editing symbols, move on to review the chart.

Teaching the Lesson

Sixteen Symbols

Extend the discussion you had in Setting Up the Lesson by reviewing the chart, symbol by symbol. You can go as quickly as your students' understanding permits, but encourage questions. If any symbol is confusing, provide an additional example on the overhead or on the board. It is helpful for students to write out their own examples and practice using the symbols appropriately as you go along. (This exercise is for practice only; do not collect or assess it.) Tell students that the chart will be used in this lesson and again in Lesson 24.

Warming Up with Symbols

In this part of the lesson, students practice "reading" editing symbols to make sure they know what each one means. Emphasize that they will not correct the text; the goal is to interpret the editor's intent. Students should look at each sample, decide what the editing symbols mean, and then write the directions indicated by the symbols on the lines provided. Remind the class to refer to the editing symbols chart as necessary. When students have finished, partners may share their work. Next, review each of the samples to be sure that everyone is on track. You may wish to put these samples on the overhead so that you can point to the various symbols as you discuss them. Here are the two samples with corrections made and marked in boldface:

Sample 1

"When are **we going** to be there**?"**

whined Kevin from the back seat.

"**I**'m really tired and I have to go to the

bathroom.**"**

The symbols tell the writer/editor to insert quotation marks before *when,* to capitalize the first letter in *When,* to add the word *we* before *going,* to close up the letters in *going,* to insert a question mark after *there,* to capitalize the pronoun *I* in *I'm,* to insert an apostrophe in *I'm,* and to add the closing quotation marks following the word *bathroom.*

Sample 2

Our poor tomato plants **looked** as though th**e**y were about to die**.** We **h**ad been gone only **t**hree days (but **i**t had be**e**n over 100 **degrees** each day)**.**

The coded message tells the writer/editor to change *Are* to *Our,* to close up the letters in *looked,* to change the "a" to an "e" in *they,* to add a period after *die,* to make the *H* in *had* lowercase, to make the *T* in *three* lowercase, to make the *I* in *it* lowercase, to change the a to *e* in *been,* to change *degrease* to *degrees,* and to add a period after the closing parenthesis.

Share and Compare

Allow time for student partners to compare responses. Then review both samples, making sure students have interpreted each symbol correctly. For symbols that are confusing, provide additional samples and refer to the chart of editing symbols for confirmation.

Editing with Symbols

Now, students become the editors. Have them read "Traffic Jam Destiny" silently to get an idea of the number and types of errors the text contains. Then, tell students to use the chart of editing symbols for reference as they edit the passage, inserting symbols as necessary. Students should work independently first, and then compare their work with a partner's or with your corrected version. They should find a total of 30 errors. Here is the sample with editing symbols correctly placed:

Traffic Jam Destiny

I dont kn ow what it is about my mom but she has alot of bad luck as a driver. Let me give you a few examples of here bad luck. To get to my drum teachers house we have togo dwon a vary busy street, the kind that has a traffic light at every block. Whenever were running a few minutes late, her bad luck kicks in and we become a red light magnt I swear that some lights see use coming and swtich from green to red with out even a bit of yellow in between. We always seem to find every road that is under Construction as well. Roads that just moments before were probably free and clear spot us moving twoard them and instantly jam up with orange cones and large excavating equipment. On top of all this, my mom attracts every train and slow-moving vehicle out there. Eventually, we always get where we're going.

Before seeing your corrected version, student partners should compare their work. Did they find the same errors? About the same number of errors? The same types of errors? Ask whether all students used the same editing symbols in marking the text. After this discussion, share your edited version from the Teacher's Guide. You may wish to put it on an overhead transparency. Encourage students to ask questions about symbols or corrections they overlooked or do not understand. Did anyone find additional errors (beyond the 30 we identified)? Sometimes students get overzealous and mark changes that are not actually corrections, but stylistic alterations. If this should happen, take time to clarify the issue.

Extending the Lesson

- Put "Traffic Jam Destiny" on an overhead, and ask students to identify the errors and tell you how to mark them. Compare your final edited version with the one students dictated. Are the same errors marked in both versions? If not, be sure to discuss any differences.
- Make an editing symbols poster to display in your classroom. Include all of the editing symbols with which your students are familiar. The writing handbook, *Write Source 2000* (referenced on Teacher's Guide page 96), has a chart of editing symbols. You can also find such a chart in any good dictionary.
- Ask student partners to create and exchange short, faulty passages. Each student will use editing symbols to make corrections and then check with the original writer to determine whether all errors were detected and marked.

Lesson 24

The Editing Express Lane

For use with pages 104–107 in the Student Traitbook

Knowing how to read editing symbols is a good start, but students need to know how to *use* them as well. As students work on applying editing symbols to faulty text, two things happen. First, they become more skilled as editors—they spot errors quickly and correct them easily. Second, their increased awareness causes them to make fewer errors in their own work. In this lesson, students will continue to practice applying their editorial skills to samples in the Student Traitbook and to their own writing.

Objectives

Students will edit two writing samples, marking each for corrections, and provide an accurate error count.

Skills Focus

- Recalling editing symbols
- Applying appropriate editing symbols to faulty text
- Comparing editorial work with that of a partner
- Reflecting on personal editorial skills and setting goals

Time Frame

Allow about 50 minutes for this lesson.

Setting Up the Lesson

The purpose of this lesson is twofold: recalling editing symbols, and using an "editor's eye" to spot errors in another's text. Set up the lesson by reminding students to use the chart of editing symbols from Lesson 23 (page 101 of the Student Traitbook). Then, talk about which types of errors are easy to spot and which types are more difficult to find. Pay special attention to those problems that students identify as difficult. Watch for those in the practice ahead.

> *"Good writing is essentially rewriting."*
>
> —Roald Dahl

Teaching the Lesson

Warming Up to the Job

This portion of the lesson requires students to mark a piece of faulty text with editing symbols and to count the total number of errors. Remind students not to correct errors—just mark and count them. Following is an edited sample, showing the errors we have identified:

Moving From one city to another is hard but whne the new city is in a different state as well, moving can make it even harder. My mom recently got an important job promotion. To get the promotion we had to move from Eagle, Idaho, to Rockwall, texas. Before we made the big move, we flew to Texas to get a feel for our new twon and to look for a house

It turns out that Eagel and Rockwall aren't totally different. Eagle is close to Boise, a large city; and Rockwall is close to Dallas, and even big ger city. But thats about as close as they come to being similar. Eagle has Mountains that are close buy; you can see them from my old house. Rockwall has a water tower that you can sea from the drive way of the house my mom liked. You no how it is nothing compares to what your used to It will be OK as soon as Learn to speak Texan.

My Review

In this follow-up to the editing practice, students will record how many errors they found and how many different editing symbols they used. These numbers indicate how many different kinds of mistakes the writer made.

Share the following totals only after students have conferred with their partners.

The number of errors is **23.** Students' totals should be close to this number (within five). Approximately twelve different symbols are used.

Students are also asked to rate the sample according to how ready it is for "Express Checkout." We rate it as "nowhere close."

Now student partners may share and compare their totals. If their numbers differ by more than three, partners should review the text to see what one partner spotted that the other missed. Then, ask each pair for a final total based on their combined counts. This number should be at or very near our total of 26. You may wish to make an overhead of the corrected text to review with students.

Getting Better

Most students will find this practice more challenging than those they have done previously. The text is long and contains many errors, including faulty paragraphing. Tell students to take their time, first reading silently, then aloud—and then a third time to check for any errors they may have overlooked. Students should work individually at first; time for partners to compare will come later. Remind students to record the number and types of errors and to review the text a final time: is it ready for Express Checkout?

Following is an edited version:

my parents alsways told me that the the reason they liked to travel so muych was because every where they went they learned something about their own lives by learning about how other People lived. of cours e, this was also the reason they took us on soo many trips with them I dont know if I always learned new things abbut my life, but I did see alot of amazing and sometimes, strange things. about a year ago, we were driving through some of the states that didn't have any Pins in them my dad liked to place pins with little flags on this map to show all the places we've been.

North Dakota was one of the states without any pins. nothing against north Dakota, but it's not exactly the place vacationers think of When they plan a trip.

All I really knew about North Dakota wa sthat it often had the coldest winter Temperatures, in the United States and that it was above South DAkota. we where driving through threw the middle of nowhere when we came upon this little town this little town right around dinner time. There were only two restaurants one was a coffee shop and the other was an italian place, my dad's choice. We all kind of laughed at the idea of finding an Italina restaurant in this little town in north Dakota the man who led us to our table said, "Welcome to Napolitano's, a little slice of Italy just for you then he shouted something in Italian to another man who had poked his head out of the kitchen door.

I knew this was the kind of place my parents would love.

My Review

Students should indicate how many errors they found and how many different editing symbols they used. The counts will be quite high. Share the following totals after student partners have conferred.

The total number of errors is **46.** Student totals should be the same or within five of this number. The number of different symbols is approximately **15.** As before, students will rate the sample according to how ready it is for "Express Checkout." We rate this one as "nowhere close."

Student partners should share and compare their totals. If their numbers differ by more than three or four, they should review the text to find what one partner spotted that the other missed. Ask each pair for a final total based on their combined counts. You may wish to make an overhead of the corrected text to review with students.

Extending the Lesson

- If you have not already done so, share the edited versions of the text with students. Distribute individual copies or use an overhead transparency to review the text, and discuss any errors about which students disagree.
- Ask students to do similar editing on text of their own. If the text is on file, they should make sure that it is double-spaced and then print it out for editing. Remind students that large margins provide additional space for editing.
- Encourage student partners to exchange and review each other's edited work. Point out that an extra pair of eyes *always* helps.
- Identify students who are especially adept in resolving a particular type of editing problem: spelling, punctuation, dialogue, effective paragraphing, and so on. While the class is editing, invite these students to set up a consultation area. Remind the consultants that they are not to do all the editing for other students. Their purpose is to offer advice and encouragement.
- When you or your students come upon a book, anthology, or poetry collection that is especially well edited, draft a letter to the editor commenting on his or her work, and ask for editing tips. Compare what the editors have to say with students' "common sense" tips for editing.
- Volunteer your students' services as editors for special projects: school documents, letters of various types, lunch menus, posters or notices, newsletter copy, or any parent or community projects. Assign students to work in teams. Remind them to be particularly meticulous because the final product will be shared with the public. When students have finished, discuss the special demands of real-world editing.

Conventions

Teacher's Guide pages 95, 180–191
Transparency numbers 21–24

Objective

Students will review and apply what they have learned about the trait of conventions.

Reviewing Conventions

Review with students what they have learned about the trait of conventions. Ask students to discuss what conventions are and to explain why conventions are important in a piece of writing. Then ask them to recall the main points about conventions that are discussed in Unit 6. Students' responses should include the following points:

- Understand the differences between revising and editing.
- Spot errors in faulty text.
- Recognize and apply 16 editor's symbols.
- Use a personal editing checklist.

Applying Conventions

To help students apply what they have learned about the trait of conventions, distribute copies of the Student Rubric for conventions on page 95 of this Teacher's Guide. Students will use these to score one or more of the sample papers that begin on page 116. The papers for conventions are also on overhead transparencies 21–24.

Before students score the papers, explain that a rubric is a grading system that determines the score a piece of writing should receive for a particular trait. Preview the Student Rubric for Conventions, pointing out that a paper very strong in conventions receives a score of 6 and a paper very weak in conventions receives a score of 1. Tell students to read the rubric and then read the paper they will score. Then tell them to look at the paper and the rubric together to determine the score the paper should receive. Encourage students to make notes on each paper to help them score it. For example, they might use editor's symbols to note errors.

The wrap-up activities in this section are designed for students who have worked with all six traits of writing.

Wrap-up Activity 1 should take about 12 minutes, Activity 2 about 10 minutes, and Activity 3 about 20 minutes. Each activity may be completed on separate days, and are not meant to be graded.

Wrap-up Activity 1

Tips & Speed Bumps

For use with Student Traitbook pages 108–109

For this activity, students should feel free to refer to Sample Papers or any personal notes. The idea is to determine what they have internalized about each of the traits. Using their own words, they should provide tips for success and "speed bumps" to look out for—they should not copy the wording from the rubrics. In fact, they should NOT refer directly to the rubrics until they have finished their own analyses.

After students have completed their work, ask teams to present their ideas to the class. You may wish to call on more than one team per trait. Invite class members to ask questions and offer comments. Use your own judgment or refer to the Teacher Rubrics to ensure that students' responses are on target.

Wrap-up Activity 2

Spotting a Problem

For use with Student Traitbook pages 110–111

The purpose of this lesson is to see whether students can identify the "problem trait" within each of four short paragraphs. A given paragraph may have more than one problem, but students should have little difficulty spotting the most significant problem.

Suggested Answers

Sample 1

The MAIN problem with this paragraph is weak **sentence fluency.** Most of the sentences are the same length, creating a monotonous rhythm that will put a reader to sleep.

Sample 2

The MAIN problem with this paragraph is lack of **voice.** This writer has an excellent opportunity to make readers experience her fear, but instead she restates the obvious: it was scary.

Sample 3

The MAIN problem with this paragraph is weak **ideas.** This writer tells us almost nothing specific at all. Who is the famous author? What sort of books does she write?

Sample 4

The MAIN problem with this paragraph is the lack of **organization.** The information is presented in a manner that requires the reader to reread the information to make sense of it.

Wrap-up Activity 3

Making a Diagnosis

For use with Student Traitbook pages 111–112

To assess and revise their own writing, students must be able to review any sample of writing and identify its strengths and weaknesses. Distribute copies of the rubrics for all six traits. Then have each student score "The Storyteller" on the six traits. When students have finished scoring, have student partners compare their scores. Finally, discuss the results with the entire class, asking students to justify scores by referring to the rubrics.

Suggested Scores and Rationales

Ideas: 5

"The Storyteller" has a clear main idea. (Grandma told good stories based on her unusual life experiences.) Most of the details in the paper relate to this main idea, and they are certainly based on the writer's personal knowledge and insight. There is one confusing point: Which story is the writer's favorite? This confusion may cause some students to drop the ideas score to a 4.

Organization: 4

The first paragraph sets the stage well, but the writer takes too much time getting to the main point. The conclusion also feels a little abrupt. In addition, the writer wanders from the main topic with the undeveloped paragraph about Rufus, the comments on current traffic, and drinking coffee.

Voice: 4

The writer seems engaged through most of the paper, especially when she tells about the killing of the rattlesnake. On the other hand, the voice fades significantly at times, such as when the writer is trying to recall her age at the time of the story and again at the conclusion when readers might like to hear more of the rattlesnake story.

Word Choice: 3

The word choice is functional and occasionally strong, but these moments are rare. Much of the language is fairly ordinary. Stronger verbs and more original phrasing would help.

Sentence Fluency: 6

Sentence beginnings and lengths are highly varied. Reading the paper aloud makes it clear that this is the most effective trait of this paper.

Conventions: 5

This writer has done reasonably careful editing. With the exception of a few errors (can your students spot them?), spelling, punctuation, paragraphing, and capitals are correct.

Contents

Sample Papers: Introduction

The purpose of the Sample Papers is to help students view each trait as a whole. By learning to evaluate a piece of writing, students will become better revisers and writers. This Sample Papers section contains copymasters of Sample Papers. There are four Sample Papers for each trait, twenty-four papers in all. Each sample paper is also on an overhead transparency. For each trait, you will find two fairly strong papers and two weaker (in process) papers. The Teacher's Guide will give you suggested scores and a rationale for a particular perspective on every paper.

Using the Sample Papers

You can use each paper alone, for which you need to allow about 20 minutes (the approximate time required to read, score, and discuss one paper). As an alternative, you can use the papers in pairs, in which case you need to allow at least 40 minutes. You must decide whether your students can focus their attention for such an extended discussion. If you decide to use papers in pairs, we strongly recommend that you select one strong paper and one weak paper to provide contrast.

It is important to present the traits in the order in which they appear in the Student Traitbook and in the Teacher's Guide. You may, however, present the four papers for an individual trait in any order you wish. Read in advance all four papers for the trait at hand, and decide how you will present them. This will also give you time to become familiar with the papers before discussing them with your class.

In advance

- Read the paper aloud *to yourself* so that you know it well and are prepared to share it with students.

At the time of the lesson

- Remind students about key points they should be looking or listening for in response to a particular paper (trait). Keep this list *short.* (Tips for each paper are given in the Teacher's Guide.)
- Read the paper to your students, using as much inflection as the text allows. Some papers have a lot of voice, and some have very little. Be enthusiastic, but don't "invent" voice where it does not exist. (about 1–2 minutes)
- Have students reflect on the relative strengths or weaknesses of a paper. (about 4–5 minutes)
- Ask students to commit *in writing* the score a paper should receive for a given trait. Do *not* share your own opinion yet. (1 minute)
- If you use hard copies of the papers, students may be asked to perform simple tasks such as underlining favorite words or circling overused words. Allow time for this activity before discussing each paper. (about 1–2 minutes)
- Ask students to compare responses with a partner. Have them answer a question such as *Why do you think this paper is strong in ideas?* (about 3–4 minutes)
- When partners have finished talking, discuss the paper with the class as a whole. Ask how many students considered the paper strong and how many considered it weak. Record the numbers and compare them. (2 minutes)
- Lead a full-class discussion. Ask students to justify their decisions: Why did they think the paper was strong or weak? Suggested questions for each paper are provided in the Teacher's Guide. (5 minutes or less)

Sample Papers

IDEAS

Paper 1: If I Were Stranded (Score: 6)*
Paper 2: Energy—A Problem! (Score: 3)
Paper 3: The Most Beautiful Thing (Score: 3)
Paper 4: Sea Horses (Score: 6)

ORGANIZATION

Paper 5: My Idea of Art (Score: 2)
Paper 6: Camping? No Thanks! (Score: 6)
Paper 7: Monster (Score: 3)
Paper 8: Insects—Learn to Love Them! (Score: 5)

VOICE

Paper 9: Maps (Score: 3)
Paper 10: A Gift for Giving (Score: 4)
Paper 11: Miss Obnoxious (Score: 6)
Paper 12: Tornado (Score: 2)

WORD CHOICE

Paper 13: Mature Audiences Only (Score: 6)
Paper 14: Having Braces (Score: 3)
Paper 15: Planting Tomatoes (Score: 2)
Paper 16: Go with the Flow! (Score: 4)

SENTENCE FLUENCY

Paper 17: Mosquitoes, Beware! (Score: 3)
Paper 18: Hold the Garlic, Please! (Score: 6)
Paper 19: It's for You (Score: 5)
Paper 20: Moving (Score: 2)

CONVENTIONS

Paper 21: Handling Food Carefully (Score: 2)
Paper 22: Worms—They're Everywhere (Score: 4)
Paper 23: Golf Mania (Score: 6)
Paper 24: Why Do I Need a Job? (Score: 3)

*See the Appendix, beginning on page 192, for using a 5-point rubric.

Sample Paper 1: If I Were Stranded

Objective

Students will learn that a strong main point, well supported with examples and details, makes a paper strong in ideas.

Materials

Student Rubric for Ideas (Teacher's Guide page 5)
Sample Paper 1: If I Were Stranded (Teacher's Guide page 122 and/or Overhead 1)

Scoring the Paper

1. Distribute copies of the sample paper and the Student Rubric for Ideas. Use the rubric to focus students' attention on the key features of the trait of IDEAS—main idea and details. Review the concept of a detail as important or interesting information that helps explain or expand the main idea.
2. Have students think about these questions as they listen to you read the paper: *Does the writer stay focused on the main topic (what to take if you were stranded on a desert island)? Does the writer provide enough information to help a reader understand which choices make sense and which do not? Is the reader left with any questions?*
3. Ask students to score the paper individually, using the rubric. They should mark their scores in writing, putting an **X** in the appropriate blank. (If students do not have copies of the sample paper, they can write on separate sheets of paper.)
4. Ask students to compare their responses with those of a partner. They should take a few minutes to talk about the paper and ask each other questions. Expect this process to be slow at first; they will talk more and come to agreement faster over time.
5. After three or four minutes, ask students to share their reasons for scoring the paper as they did.

Discussing the Paper

Discuss the paper with the class. Ask students to say what scores they gave the paper and why. The *why* is the most important part in deepening their understanding. Use the following questions to encourage discussion:

- What is the writer's main idea? Can you express it in your own words?
- Does the writer provide enough information to support the idea that a fishing rod would be the best thing to take along if you were stranded on an island? Do you agree with the writer's conclusion? Why?
- Which are the most important or interesting details in the piece?
- Do the details suggest that this writer has really thought about this topic?

*Rationale for the Score**

Most students should see this paper as **strong.** It received a score of **6,** based on the 6-point rubric. This writing has a clear main idea, and the writer never loses focus on that main idea. The writer gives reasons for his or her choice and also explores (briefly) the folly of other possible choices. Without putting in too many details, the writer explains that fishing could be entertaining and that it could relieve loneliness and boredom while sharpening other skills. The ironic twist at the end is a nice touch.

Extensions

1. Ask each student to look at a piece of his or her own writing. Is the main idea clear? Does it remain clear all the way through? If not, what could be added or deleted to improve the clarity and focus?
2. This writer chooses an interesting pattern of organization—and you may wish to discuss this as a way of previewing an upcoming trait. He waits to tell us his choice until he has given us an idea of what he thinks of his friends' choices. Do students like this approach? Ask them whether the writer should have given his choice first and then written about the others. Have students explain how this change might affect the paper.
3. Ask students to write on this same topic. What would they take to a deserted island? Put a time limit on the visit if you wish—a month or six months. Students cannot choose a fishing rod—but they can defend one of the other choices mentioned if they wish. Remind students that originality enhances ideas.

*See Teacher's Guide page 193 for a 5-point rubric and page 205 for the score based on that rubric.

name: .... date: ....

Sample Paper 1: IDEAS

If I Were Stranded

What would you do if you were stranded on an island, and you could take only one thing with you? Now, think before you answer!

I have a lot of friends who, when asked this question, give answers such as a watch, video games, or a book. First, why would you want a watch? If you were stranded for any length of time, hours and minutes would cease to have meaning. Video games are also a poor choice. What are the chances you'd have electricity? Batteries wouldn't last long. What's more, you'd be too busy finding food and water to lie around playing video games. A book is a sensible answer. At least you would have entertainment and company. But reading the same book over and over could make you crazy. You'd be better off writing your own book.

I would take my fly-fishing rod to a deserted island. You have to eat, and if you're on an island, it stands to reason that there are fish around. I would keep myself entertained and occupied.

In short, a fishing rod is the perfect solution. After all, being stranded on an island with no distractions or competition is a dream for someone like me, who loves to fish—as long as I'm not stranded for too long!

Mark the score that this paper should receive in the trait of IDEAS.
Read your rubric for Ideas to help you decide.

____ 1 ____ 2 ____ 3 ____ 4 ____ 5 ____ 6

Sample Paper 2: Energy—A Problem!

Objective

Students will learn that although generalities may provide the basis for a message, absence of detail weakens ideas.

Materials

Student Rubric for Ideas (Teacher's Guide page 5)
Sample Paper 2: Energy—A Problem! (Teacher's Guide page 125 and/or Overhead 2)

Scoring the Paper

1. Distribute copies of the sample paper and the Student Rubric for Ideas. Use the rubric to focus students' attention on the key features of the trait of IDEAS—main idea and details. Review the concept of a detail as important or interesting information that helps explain or expand the main idea.
2. Have students think about these questions as they listen to you read the paper: *Does the paper have a strong main idea? Does the writer provide specific details or mostly generalities on the topic of energy? Is the reader left with too many questions?*
3. Ask students to score the paper individually, using the rubric. They should mark their scores in writing, putting an **X** in the appropriate blank. (If students do not have copies of the sample paper, they can write on separate sheets of paper.)
4. Ask students to compare their responses with those of a partner. They should take a few minutes to talk about the paper and ask each other questions. Expect this process to be slow at first; they will talk more and come to agreement faster over time.
5. After three or four minutes, ask students to share their reasons for scoring the paper as they did.

Discussing the Paper

Discuss the paper with the class. Ask students to say what scores they gave the paper and why. The *why* is the most important part in deepening their understanding. Use the following questions to encourage discussion:

- What is the writer's main idea? Is it easy to identify?
- Does the writer help you personalize this topic—that is, make connections to your own life or experience? Explain your response.
- Does this writer select interesting and helpful details or suggestions about the energy issue? Does he or she rely too much on generalities? Give examples.

*Rationale for the Score**

Most students should see this paper as **in process.** It received a score of **3,** based on the 6-point rubric. It is quite simple to infer this writer's main idea: we should all be concerned about energy problems. However, the writing is not focused. It deals with issues of pollution, energy sources that should or could be explored, and ways to conserve energy. The writer also introduces the topic of education early on but does not follow up. The paper tries to cover too much territory; as a result, it covers nothing in depth. The writer needs to know the topic better in order to share new, important, and interesting information.

Extensions

1. Ask students to underline generalities in this paper. How many do they find? How do they spot a generality—and distinguish it from a good, solid detail that provides new information? As a next step, you may wish to ask students to search their own writing for generalities. What does this search yield?
2. As a class, research the energy issue. Ask each person to bring in one or two striking bits of information: anecdotes, personal experiences, or facts. Post these on index cards where everyone can see them. Ask students to review this information and select three to five new details to incorporate in a revision of "Energy—A Problem!" Talk about the difference specific information makes.
3. Have students write in the "generalities only, please" mode about a topic they know well—themselves! Ask them to imagine that the author of "Energy—A Problem!" is going to write descriptions of people in your class. How might these descriptions sound? Have each student write one or two paragraphs, describing himself or herself as this author might.

*See Teacher's Guide page 193 for a 5-point rubric and page 205 for the score based on that rubric.

name: .... date: ....

Sample Paper 2: IDEAS

Energy—A Problem!

With all the talk about security measures, it's pretty easy to forget about other important problems, such as education, pollution, and energy. We cannot keep on using energy sources like gas, oil, and coal that cause pollution. If we do, we will not be able to drink our water or breathe our air! Traffic is getting worse all the time, and people worry only about gas prices going up. It would be good if prices were even higher. Then our pollution might go down because people would drive less. We also could use less energy in other ways, such as turning off lights and stuff. We could turn off our computers when we are not using them. We also could turn off lights and some appliances. Solar power could help because it does not create the same pollution as oil or gas, and it is free. We also could use wind power. There is plenty of it! Someday, we might have cars that can use other kinds of fuel, such as hydrogen. It is important to work together to solve our energy problems. If we don't, these problems will only grow worse in the future.

Mark the score that this paper should receive in the trait of IDEAS. Read your rubric for Ideas to help you decide. Then write your reason for the score.

____ 1 ____ 2 ____ 3 ____ 4 ____ 5 ____ 6

____

____

Sample Paper 3: The Most Beautiful Thing

Objective

Students will learn that writing is weaker when the writer does not explain information or develop details to paint a clear picture in the reader's mind.

Materials

Student Rubric for Ideas (Teacher's Guide page 5)
Sample Paper 3: The Most Beautiful Thing (Teacher's Guide page 128 and/or Overhead 3)

Scoring the Paper

1. Distribute copies of the sample paper and the Student Rubric for Ideas. Use the rubric to focus students' attention on the key features of the trait of IDEAS—main idea and details. Review the concept of a detail as important or interesting information that helps explain or expand the main idea.
2. Have students think about these questions as they listen to you read the paper: *Is the main idea clear? Does the writer provide details that help you picture how and why moths are beautiful? Does this writer stay focused?*
3. Ask students to score the paper individually, using the rubric. They should mark their scores in writing, putting an **X** in the appropriate blank. (If students do not have copies of the sample paper, they can write on separate sheets of paper.)
4. Ask students to compare their responses with those of a partner. They should take a few minutes to talk about the paper and ask each other questions. Expect this process to be slow at first; they will talk more and come to agreement faster over time.
5. After three or four minutes, ask students to share their reasons for scoring the paper as they did.

Discussing the Paper

Discuss the paper with the class. Ask students to say what scores they gave the paper and why. The *why* is the most important part in deepening their understanding. Use the following questions to encourage discussion:

- What is this writer's main idea? Does he or she ever wander from that main idea? If so, where and how?
- Does the writer expand his or her details to help you picture things clearly? Are there any parts where the picture grows fuzzy? If so, where?
- Does this writer know enough about this topic to write the paper? What kinds of information could make this paper stronger?

*Rationale for the Score**

Most students should see this paper as **in process.** It received a score of **3,** based on the 6-point rubric. Although the main idea (moths are beautiful creatures) is easy to infer, the writer does not paint a clear picture. Readers know that moths have colorful markings and patterns. But readers need precise, vivid descriptions. What colors? What patterns? In addition, the writer goes off-track at the end with comments about the destruction of crops and the short life of moths. This information has nothing to do with the moths' appearance. It might be possible to tie these comments to the main idea, but the writer does not do so.

Extensions

1. Ask students to sketch a moth based strictly on the writer's description. What does this moth look like? Discuss whether the writer provides enough information.
2. Give students time to examine closely any small object from the classroom. Provide magnifying glasses for this activity if possible. Ask each student to write a detailed description of what he or she sees. Then, have them exchange descriptions with partners and see whether the partners can draw what they read in each other's descriptions. Discuss results and the importance of vivid detail.
3. Invite each student to review a piece of his or her own writing for vivid detail. It need not be a descriptive piece. Students might review only a line or two of description. How do they rate the clarity of their images?

*See Teacher's Guide page 193 for a 5-point rubric and page 205 for the score based on that rubric.

name: .... date: ....

Sample Paper 3: IDEAS

The Most Beautiful Thing

Have you ever seen a moth up close? It is one of the most beautiful things you will ever see. Moths have amazing colors, colors unlike any colors that you will see elsewhere. You might see shades of blue or green, gold or brown, depending on the kind of moth. Some moths look furry or fuzzy when you see them at close range. Their antennae are totally amazing. Moth wings have a lot of unusual patterns that show up as you look at them through a magnifying glass or microscope. Maybe these patterns help the moth hide or scare off predators. Some people photograph or paint moths because they are like works of art. Of course, some people do not like moths at all and will kill them if they can. Cats kill moths, as well. Moths can do a lot of damage to crops, especially in the caterpillar stage. They lay eggs that hatch to become destructive caterpillars. Moths live only about two or three weeks at the most.

Mark the score this paper should receive in the trait of IDEAS.
Read your rubric for Ideas to help you decide.

___ 1 ___ 2 ___ 3 ___ 4 ___ 5 ___ 6

Compare your score with your partner's scores. How did you do?

___ We matched **exactly!**

___ We matched within **one point**—pretty good!

___ We were **two points or more** apart. We need to discuss this.

Sample Paper 4: Sea Horses

Objective

Students will learn that unusual, interesting, and vivid details make a paper strong in ideas.

Materials

Student Rubric for Ideas (Teacher's Guide page 5)
Sample Paper 4: Sea Horses (Teacher's Guide page 131 and/or Overhead 4)

Scoring the Paper

1. Distribute copies of the sample paper and the Student Rubric for Ideas. Use the rubric to focus students' attention on the key features of the trait of IDEAS—main idea and details. Review the concept of a detail as important or interesting information that helps explain or expand the main idea.
2. Have students think about these questions as they listen to you read the paper: *Is the main idea clear? Are details helpful, or are they too general? Does each piece of information contribute something to the paper as a whole?*
3. Ask students to score the paper individually, using the student rubric. They should mark their scores in writing, putting an **X** in the appropriate blank. (If students do not have copies of the sample paper, they can write on separate sheets of paper.)
4. Ask students to compare their responses with those of a partner. They should take a few minutes to talk about the paper and ask each other questions. Expect this process to be slow at first; they will talk more and come to agreement faster over time.
5. After three or four minutes, ask students to share their reasons for scoring the paper as they did.

Discussing the Paper

Discuss the paper with the class. Ask students to say what scores they gave the paper and why. The *why* is the most important part in deepening their understanding. Use the following questions to encourage discussion:

- What do you learn about sea horses from this paper?
- What is the main idea of this paper? Does the writer state it directly?
- Does this paper read like an encyclopedia entry—or is it different? If so, how?

*Rationale for the Score**

Most students should see this paper as **strong.** It received a **6,** based on the 6-point rubric. It is highly focused and has a strong main idea: the sea horse is a fragile, unusual creature that needs protection to survive. Everything in the paper relates to this idea (which is never directly stated). This paper is a good example of what sound informational writing should be. It informs the reader by presenting a rich array of details. Though this writer shares many facts, they are not piled on in encyclopedic fashion; for example, the image of the sea horse sucking up food like a tiny vacuum cleaner paints a vivid and lively picture. This paper would likely score high in voice as well.

Extensions

1. List specific facts that you or your students learned from this paper. Often, the strength of an informational piece can be measured—at least in part—by the amount of new information gained.
2. Have students look up the term "sea horse" in the encyclopedia and read what they find (or part of it) aloud. Have them compare "Sea Horses" with the encyclopedia entry. Which is more informative? Which is more appealing? Why?
3. This writer makes good use of similes. See how many of these students can find. Discuss how similes add to the quality of detail in this piece.

*See Teacher's Guide page 193 for a 5-point rubric and page 206 for the score based on that rubric.

name: .... date: ....

Sample Paper 4: IDEAS

Sea Horses

The sea horse is a delicate and unique creature. It is not a horse at all, of course, but a fish, though its head resembles the head of a horse. It belongs to the genus Hippocampus. Hippocampus was a figure from Greek mythology that was half horse and half fish.

The sea horse does not have scales, as most fish do. Its skin is stretched tight as a drum over bony plates beneath and can change color, which lets it hide from enemies. The sea horse uses its long, curly tail to hook onto ocean plants when it wants to hide. To swim, it uses powerful dorsal fins that beat almost as fast as a hummingbird's wings. The really interesting part is that it swims upright, like a figure on a carousel, not stretched out like other fish.

Everything about the little sea horse is unusual, but most unusual of all is the fact that it is the male who gives birth! The female deposits eggs into the male's brood pouch, and after 10 to 30 days, the male gives birth to as many as 1,000 babies! That sounds like a lot (and it is), but only a very few survive into adulthood. Hong Kong, Taiwan, and some parts of Europe have set up sanctuaries for the sea horse or made laws outlawing its capture. If we are lucky, such measures will protect this unusual and frail sea creature.

Mark the score that this paper should receive in the trait of IDEAS. Read your rubric for Ideas to help you decide.

___ 1 ___ 2 ___ 3 ___ 4 ___ 5 ___ 6

Sample Paper 5: My Idea of Art

Objective

Students will learn that disjointed observations that do not connect to a main idea create a serious problem with organization.

Materials

Student Rubric for Organization (Teacher's Guide page 23)
Sample Paper 5: My Idea of Art (Teacher's Guide page 134 and/or Overhead 5)

Scoring the Paper

1. Distribute copies of the sample paper and the Student Rubric for Organization. Use the rubric to focus students' attention on the key features of ORGANIZATION—a strong lead and conclusion, effective transitions, and an organizational sequence or pattern that is easy to follow.
2. Have students think about these questions as they listen to you read the paper: *Is the paper easy to follow? Does it begin and end effectively? Is it easy to connect ideas in your mind?*
3. Ask students to score the paper individually, using the rubric. They should mark their scores in writing, putting an **X** in the appropriate blank. (If students do not have copies of the sample paper, they can write on separate sheets of paper.)
4. Ask students to compare their responses with those of a partner. They should take a few minutes to talk about the paper and ask each other questions. Expect this process to be slow at first; they will talk more and come to agreement faster over time.
5. After three or four minutes, ask students to share their reasons for scoring the paper as they did.

Discussing the Paper

Discuss the paper with the class. Ask students to say what scores they gave the paper and why. The *why* is the most important part in deepening their understanding. Use the following questions to encourage discussion:

- Do you like the lead for this paper? Why?
- Do you like the conclusion? Why?
- Is this paper easy to follow? Do the ideas seem closely connected—or somewhat random, more like loose marbles in a bag?
- Are the transitions (words or phrases that connect ideas) strong or weak?

*Rationale for the Score**

Most students should see this paper as **in process.** It received a score of **2,** based on the 6-point rubric, because the observations are randomly made rather than closely connected. The lead is indefinite: what is meant by "weird stuff"? The conclusion is a platitude: art is important to the world. The paper does not support this conclusion. With the exception of architecture, the writer does not seem to care much about art. The writer first needs to define his or her topic and then stick with it, connecting all details to the main idea as well as to each other.

Extensions

1. This writer seems to feel strongly about the importance of architecture to the world of art. What if he or she had begun with that idea? Tell students to craft some new leads that focus on this portion of the writer's paper. Then have them compare these new leads with what the writer actually wrote. What differences do they see and hear?
2. A well-organized piece of writing should be as easy to follow as a good road map. Ask students to read through this piece thoughtfully and to put an X in the margin each time the "map" becomes a little hard to read. How many Xs do students mark? Where do the Xs occur? Now, ask students to use this same exercise with their own writing. Tell them to revise as necessary.

*See Teacher's Guide page 194 for a 5-point rubric and page 206 for the score based on that rubric.

name: .... date: ....

Sample Paper 5: ORGANIZATION

My Idea of Art

What is art? If you go to an art museum, you can see some pretty weird stuff. You can see some really neat stuff, too, like paintings from other cultures or from other times. Art can show how other people see the world. Once I saw a painting (maybe it was a sculpture) that was just a board painted blue, and it had the title "Blue." Our teacher said to imagine what this made us think about. What it made me think was that if that blue board was art, then anything could be art.

My father mostly likes art that looks like what it is supposed to be, such as a painting of a house, a person, or an animal. My mom likes art that makes her think of other things. In a museum you can see art of many different types from many historical times. The museum I go to has a lot more art that would appeal to my mom than to my dad.

For example, I think the greatest art in the world is architecture. I also think Frank Lloyd Wright was a great architect. You can look at any kind of architecture for a long time. Architecture is not like a painting that you get tired of after it hangs on your wall for a while. It takes a lot longer to build a building than to paint a board. Art should take time.

Mark the score that this paper should receive in the trait of ORGANIZATION. Read your rubric for Organization to help you decide.

____ 1 ____ 2 ____ 3 ____ 4 ____ 5 ____ 6

Sample Paper 6: Camping? No Thanks!

Objective

Students will learn that a strong lead and conclusion plus effective sequencing of ideas make for strong organization.

Materials

Student Rubric for Organization (Teacher's Guide page 23)
Sample Paper 6: Camping? No Thanks! (Teacher's Guide page 137 and/or Overhead 6)

Scoring the Paper

1. Distribute copies of the sample paper and the Student Rubric for Organization. Use the rubric to focus students' attention on the key features of the trait of ORGANIZATION—a strong lead and conclusion, effective transitions, and an organizational pattern that is easy to follow.
2. Have students think about these questions as they listen to you read the paper: *Does the paper have an identifiable pattern? Is it easy to follow? Does it have a strong lead and conclusion?*
3. Ask students to score the paper individually, using the student rubric. They should mark their scores in writing, putting an **X** in the appropriate blank. (If students do not have copies of the sample paper, they can write on separate sheets of paper.)
4. Ask students to compare their responses with those of a partner. They should take a few minutes to talk about the paper and ask each other questions.
5. After three or four minutes, ask students to share their reasons for scoring the paper as they did.

Discussing the Paper

Discuss the paper with the class. Ask students to say what scores they gave the paper and why. The *why* is the most important part in deepening their understanding. Use the following questions to encourage discussion:

- Does this paper have a strong lead? Why do you think so?
- Does it have a strong conclusion? Why do you think so?
- Is the paper easy to follow? Does the writer stick to his or her key points or does the paper wander from the topic?
- Do strong transitions connect key points or parts of the paper? Can you point to an example?

*Rationale for the Score**

Most students should see this paper as **strong.** It received a score of **6,** based on the 6-point rubric, because it has a very strong lead and conclusion and is easy to follow. The writer follows a definite time-order pattern, wrapping up with conclusions about how he or she feels. The transitions are especially strong: *Camping starts . . . This is the part . . . Later, when we're around the campfire . . .* The writer uses the notation "Part II: On the Trail" to introduce one segment of the paper, but this strategy is inconsistent throughout the paper. However, the designation does not disrupt the flow of ideas.

Extensions

1. What transitional phrases or words do students find? Have them underline these terms and discuss this writer's use of transitions. Ask students to check their own writing to see how strong their transitions are. Ask them to explain why transitions are so important.
2. Was the conclusion what students expected? Have students write different conclusions in which the writer has a different attitude. Which conclusion is most effective?
3. What if the first paragraph were deleted? Would this strengthen or weaken the paper? Why? Ask students to try this with a piece of their own work. Tell them to delete the first paragraph or begin in a different spot. What difference does this change make?

*See Teacher's Guide page 194 for a 5-point rubric and page 207 for the score based on that rubric.

name: .... date: ....

Sample Paper 6: ORGANIZATION

Camping? No Thanks!

What is the most overrated activity in America? If you said camping, you win the prize. Now, don't get me wrong. If people really enjoy camping, that's okay. Just don't invite me along.

Camping starts with packing. My dad always says, "Bring only what you need." Is he kidding? Everything I need is right here at home. I can bring only what fits in one small backpack, a pack I'll be carrying over miles of rough trails. But if I had a pack mule to haul a TV, a computer, and a sleeping bag big enough to let me unbend my knees when I sleep, I would be happier.

Part II: On the Trail

This is the part where we hike to our campsite. Other people drive to campsites where they pitch tents in shady spots. I see them as we're driving to the trailhead, and it always makes me jealous. They cook their hot dogs while we hike to some remote trail in search of the perfect campsite.

Later, when we're around the campfire roasting the marshmallows and listening to the wind in the trees, I almost like camping. I know that I won't see a bathroom for days and that I have to endure 10,000 more mosquitoes, but seeing the smile on my dad's face makes me feel good.

Mark the score that this paper should receive in the trait of ORGANIZATION. Read your rubric for Organization to help you decide.

___ 1 ___ 2 ___ 3 ___ 4 ___ 5 ___ 6

Sample Paper 7: Monster

Objective

Students will learn that even when a writer has a lot to say, the information must be presented in logical, effective order if it is to have clarity and impact.

Materials

Student Rubric for Organization (Teacher's Guide page 23)
Sample Paper 7: Monster (Teacher's Guide page 140 and/or Overhead 7)

Scoring the Paper

1. Distribute copies of the sample paper and the Student Rubric for Organization. Use the rubric to focus students' attention on the key features of ORGANIZATION—a strong lead and conclusion, effective transitions, and an organizational pattern that is easy to follow.
2. Have students think about these questions as they listen to you read the paper: *Does this paper have an identifiable pattern? Is it easy to follow, or are the ideas presented at random? Does the paper have a strong lead and conclusion?*
3. Ask students to score the paper individually, using the student rubric. They should mark their scores in writing, putting an **X** in the appropriate blank. (If students do not have copies of the sample paper, they can write on separate sheets of paper.)
4. Ask students to compare their responses with those of a partner. They should take a few minutes to talk about the paper and ask each other questions.
5. After three or four minutes, ask students to share their reasons for scoring the paper as they did.

Discussing the Paper

Discuss the paper with the class. Ask students to say what scores they gave the paper and why. The *why* is the most important part in deepening their understanding. Use the following questions to encourage discussion:

- Is this paper easy to follow? Do you need to reread to understand the writer's message? Does the writer surprise you by saying things that don't follow from what was said previously?
- Do you like the lead? If not, how would you change it?
- Do you like the conclusion? Would you change it? In what way?
- Are the paper's points carefully connected, like links in a chain? Can you point to a spot where the chain is weak or broken?

*Rationale for the Score**

Most students should see this paper as **in process.** It received a score of **3,** based on the 6-point rubric, because the lead is weak, the conclusion just stops, and the order is poor. Transitions are weak, but this is not surprising because the paper leaps from point to point without connecting ideas. In addition, the writer offers unnecessary details (wandering around the park, getting scared when skiing). The paper could be condensed. Because the second half of the paper shows more organization than the first, the score was raised from a 2 to a 3.

Extensions

1. Both the lead and the conclusion of "Monster" need work. Ask students to rewrite either or both and share results. Read the revisions aloud. What do they illustrate about good leads or conclusions?
2. This paper should be condensed. Ask students to do this and see who can come up with the most condensed version without eliminating important ideas.
3. Both point of view and voice can influence organization. Ask students to rewrite the paper from K.C.'s point of view. Where do *these* revisions begin and end? What points in the story receive the most emphasis? What gets eliminated? How does the whole piece differ from the original?

*See Teacher's Guide page 194 for a 5-point rubric and page 207 for the score based on that rubric.

name: .... date: ....

Sample Paper 7: ORGANIZATION

Monster

My best friend K.C. said she wanted to go to the amusement park. This was on a Saturday, and there was not that much to do anyhow. I could have done my homework, but I decided to go with her.

So we just walked around for a while and ate cotton candy and elephant ears and stuff like that. I kept thinking we might meet some friends, but we didn't. K.C. wanted to go on the roller coaster. I didn't want to go because I am terrified of heights, and wild rides make me sick. We had eaten quite a bit! So we just wandered some more and then it was almost time for us to leave, so I told her I would ride the coaster. We were strapped in, and then we were flying through the air. The only other time I was that scared was when I was eight and my mom took me skiing. Later, K.C. said I was screaming the whole way, but I don't remember any of it. K.C. wanted us to ride again, but I told her no way! She rode by herself. I think some day I might go on that ride again, but maybe not. K.C.'s mom drove us home after that. By the way, in case you haven't guessed, the ride was called the "Monster."

Mark the score that this paper should receive in the trait of ORGANIZATION. Read your rubric for Organization to help you decide.

____ 1 ____ 2 ____ 3 ____ 4 ____ 5 ____ 6

Sample Paper 8: Insects—Learn to Love Them!

Objectives

Students will learn that a paper with a strong main idea tends to have strong organization.

Materials

Student Rubric for Organization (Teacher's Guide page 23)
Sample Paper 8: Insects—Learn to Love Them! (Teacher's Guide page 143 and/or Overhead 8)

Scoring the Paper

1. Distribute copies of the sample paper and the Student Rubric for Organization. Use the rubric to focus students' attention on the key features of ORGANIZATION—a strong lead and conclusion, strong focus on a main idea, effective transitions, and an organizational pattern that is easy to follow.
2. Have students think about these questions as they listen to you read the paper: *Is this paper easy to follow? Does the writer focus on his or her main idea throughout? Does the paper have a strong lead and conclusion?*
3. Ask students to score the paper individually, using the student rubric. They should mark their scores in writing, putting an **X** in the appropriate blank. (If students do not have copies of the sample paper, they can write on separate sheets of paper.)
4. Ask students to compare their responses with those of a partner. They should take a few minutes to talk about the paper and ask each other questions. Expect this process to be slow at first; they will talk more and come to agreement faster over time.
5. After three or four minutes, ask students to share their reasons for scoring the paper as they did.

Discussing the Paper

Discuss the paper with the class. Ask students to say what scores they gave the paper and why. The *why* is the most important part in deepening their understanding. Use the following questions to encourage discussion:

- Do you like the lead? Why? Does the lead set up the rest of the paper well?
- Is the conclusion effective? Why?
- Does the writer ever wander from the topic? If so, where?
- Are all of the transitions strong? Should any of them be made stronger?

*Rationale for the Score**

Most students should see this paper as **strong.** It received a score of **5,** based on the 6-point rubric, because it begins and ends effectively. Transitions are strong, too, though the connection between the second and third paragraph could be improved. The writer moves abruptly from stating that humans are not able to live without insects to claiming that humans believe that they control the earth; the two ideas are related, but the writer does not make the link clear. The paper is well focused, however, and centers consistently on this main idea: insects, though pesky, help keep us alive.

Extensions

1. Tell students to revise the paper to strengthen the transition between the second and third paragraphs. Read revisions aloud and discuss them. What changes are necessary?
2. Ask students to rewrite the piece, using paragraph three as the lead. What difference does this change make to the paper as a whole?
3. Have students rewrite this paper as an "Ode to Insects." What key bits of information do they borrow from the original essay?
4. Ask students whether the writer proves the point that insects probably will be on earth longer than humans will. Why or why not? Is this an effective conclusion?

*See Teacher's Guide page 194 for a 5-point rubric and page 207 for the score based on that rubric.

name: .... date: ....

Sample Paper 8: ORGANIZATION

Insects—Learn to Love Them!

When most people think of insects, they think, "Yuck!" After all, insects are pests, right? They bite us, causing pain and itching. They are unwelcome guests at picnics and baseball games. They gobble up our gardens. Some, especially flies and mosquitoes, carry diseases.

On the other hand, insects keep us alive—literally. They pollinate plants, providing a huge food supply for us. About one-third of a typical human's diet is directly dependent on insect pollination, especially from bees. Without the help of insects, we, and many animals, probably would starve. It is not an exaggeration to say that insects could live very well without us, but we could not exist long at all without them.

We think we control the earth because we create cities and cultures. This is an illusion, though. In fact, insects both outnumber and outweigh us. The total number of insects is about ten quintillion, which is 10 followed by seventeen zeroes! True, insects do not build cities or write books or make films or use computers, but they still adapt to life on earth much better than we do and are likely to be here longer than we will.

Mark the score that this paper should receive in the trait of ORGANIZATION. Read your rubric for Organization to help you decide.

___ 1 ___ 2 ___ 3 ___ 4 ___ 5 ___ 6

Sample Paper 9: Maps

Objective

Students will learn that personal engagement with a topic is essential to strong voice.

Materials

Student Rubric for Voice (Teacher's Guide page 41)
Sample Paper 9: Maps (Teacher's Guide page 146 and/or Overhead 9)

Scoring the Paper

1. Distribute copies of the sample paper and the Student Rubric for Voice. Use the rubric to focus students' attention on the key features of VOICE—energy, emotion, individuality, and the writer's interest in the topic and audience.
2. Have students think about these questions as they listen to you read the paper: *Is the paper lively? Is it fun to read aloud and to listen to? Would you share it? Does the writer seem engaged with the topic or bored?*
3. Ask students to score the paper individually, using the student rubric. They should mark their scores in writing, putting an **X** in the appropriate blank. (If students do not have copies of the sample paper, they can write on separate sheets of paper.)
4. Ask students to compare their responses with those of a partner. They should take a few minutes to talk about the paper and ask each other questions. Expect this process to be slow at first; they will talk more and come to agreement faster over time.
5. After three or four minutes, ask students to share their reasons for scoring the paper as they did.

Discussing the Paper

Discuss the paper with the class. Ask students to say what scores they gave the paper and why. The *why* is the most important part in deepening their understanding. Use the following questions to encourage discussion:

- Did you enjoy listening to this story? Would you like to hear more of this writer's writing? Why?
- Would you read this aloud to a friend? Why?
- Does this writer seem to enjoy telling this story? What clues do you have about how the writer feels about maps?
- Do you think this writer should have chosen another topic? Why?

*Rationale for the Score**

Most students should see this paper as **in process.** It received a score of **3,** based on the 6-point rubric. Although it has moments of strong voice, the voice is not consistently strong throughout the paper. The writer explains his or her frustration, but we do not feel the frustration. In fact, the writer sometimes sounds downright bored with the topic: *This is fun . . . Sometimes it was hard . . . Sometimes we had to stop to ask for directions . . .* These listless comments make readers feel as sleepy as if they were on a long road trip, too. The writer should become more engaged with this topic or select another topic.

Extensions

1. Sometimes adding specific examples makes a difference in voice. Ask students to rewrite this piece by inserting just **one** specific example, such as taking a wrong turn or getting lost. (They will need to invent, of course!) Tell them to have fun and to use their imaginations.
2. Invite students to review their own writing for specific details. Ask students to underline or put a check next to each generality or vague reference. Tell them to replace these with specific details and then review before and after samples for voice. What differences are there?
3. Try injecting some dialogue into this piece between the "navigator" and the driver. What impact does this have on voice? Again, students may wish to try this strategy with a piece of their own writing.

*See Teacher's Guide page 195 for a 5-point rubric and page 208 for the score based on that rubric.

name: .... date: ....

Sample Paper 9: VOICE

Maps

If I could change one thing about traveling, I would change the road maps. They are hard to read. They do not show the world the way it is in real life. This can be really frustrating.

Last summer, my family and I went on vacation to see our relatives in Nebraska. My parents took turns driving, and I got to be the navigator. They thought this would help me learn about geography. We live on the East Coast, so it was a pretty long drive. I used an atlas with a new map for each state. You just look up the state when you come to it, or if you're on an interstate, use the U.S. map. This is fun except that the real roads never match what is shown in the atlas. Sometimes it was hard to find the right road or to make sure we were going the right way. Sometimes we had to stop to ask for directions but not too often. Most of the time we could figure out the right way after a wrong turn or two. It does make you wonder whether the people who make maps actually use them. It also made me think of what a hard job mapmaking must be. When I think of all the careers in the world, mapmaking is one I definitely would not choose. One thing I'm pretty sure of, though, is that I know the way to Nebraska by heart.

Mark the score that this paper should receive in the trait of VOICE. Read your rubric for Voice to help you decide.

____ 1 ____ 2 ____ 3 ____ 4 ____ 5 ____ 6

Sample Paper 10: A Gift for Giving

Objective

Students will learn that honesty and sincerity can enhance a writer's voice but that general information can deflate voice.

Materials

Student Rubric for Voice (Teacher's Guide page 41)
Sample Paper 10: A Gift for Giving (Teacher's Guide page 149 and/or Overhead 10)

Scoring the Paper

1. Distribute copies of the sample paper and the Student Rubric for Voice. Use the rubric to focus students' attention on the key features of the trait of VOICE—energy, emotion, individuality, and the writer's interest in the topic and audience.
2. Have students think about these questions as they listen to you read the paper: *Is the paper fun to read aloud? Would you share it? Does the writer seem engaged with the topic or bored? Are some parts stronger in voice than others?*
3. Ask students to score the paper individually, using the student rubric. They should mark their scores in writing, putting an **X** in the appropriate blank. (If students do not have copies of the sample paper, they can write on separate sheets of paper.)
4. Ask students to compare their responses with those of a partner. They should take a few minutes to talk about the paper and ask each other questions.
5. After three or four minutes, ask students to share their reasons for scoring the paper as they did.

Discussing the Paper

Discuss the paper with the class. Ask students to say what scores they gave the paper and why. The *why* is the most important part in deepening their understanding. Use the following questions to encourage discussion:

- Can you tell how the writer feels about her grandmother? Where are the clues that show you?
- Are some parts of the writing stronger than others? Where are the strongest parts?
- Would you read this writing aloud to a friend? Why or why not?
- Does this writer enjoy writing about her grandmother? How can you tell?
- What changes or revisions could have made the voice even stronger?

*Rationale for the Score**

Most students should see this paper as **fairly strong.** It received a score of **4,** based on the 6-point rubric, because it is sincere and seems to be an honest tribute to a grandmother the writer obviously loves. Some parts, such as the description of the swearing on the freeway, are stronger than others. The voice fades a bit, for instance, in the conclusion. What is missing, though, is the grandmother herself. Readers cannot hear her voice. Also, although the examples are wonderful, none of them are developed. For instance, readers cannot see Shirley and the narrator reading from the mystery novel or hear them speaking. We don't get Shirley's reaction when her dog has puppies. With some dialogue and expansion of one or two examples, this paper would score better.

Extensions

1. Insert some dialogue. Let Shirley speak in two or more portions of the paper. Talk about the difference this change makes.
2. One interesting thing about Shirley is her philosophy about gifts. Ask students to expand this by capturing Shirley's point of view in a journal she might keep about some of the events the writer includes here: the birth of the puppies, kayaking, reading all night, riding in the rodeo parade.
3. Invite student writers to take one of the examples (perhaps driving on the freeway) and expand it, telling in more detail what happens and how Shirley and the writer react. Include dialogue. What difference does this make?

*See Teacher's Guide page 195 for a 5-point rubric and page 208 for the score based on that rubric.

name: .... date: ....

Sample Paper 10: VOICE

A Gift for Giving

Picture a 67-year-old woman who still swims daily, paddles a kayak, and rides in a rodeo parade. She taught me to quilt, to bake pies and biscuits, to stitch up a cut (yes, she is a doctor), and to swear. She did not mean to teach me swearing; it just happened because we ride together a lot on the freeway, the only place my grandmother Shirley shows her temper.

Of all the things Shirley has taught me, the most important is that everything we do is a gift. A smile or a song can be a gift. For my birthday last year, she taught me to paddle a kayak. The year before, I helped deliver Ginger's puppies. Ginger is her dog. One night we stayed up late reading a mystery novel aloud to each other because it was so good we couldn't put it down. Shirley even made fudge. My mom would never let me do that, so of course we didn't tell her anything about it. Shirley loves secrets almost as much as I do. She tells me I am going to make a great mother someday. I guess you could call that a gift, too, because she has helped me believe in myself.

Mark the score that this paper should receive in the trait of VOICE. Read your rubric for Voice to help you decide. Then write your reason for the score.

____ 1 ____ 2 ____ 3 ____ 4 ____ 5 ____ 6

____

____

Sample Paper 11: Miss Obnoxious

Objective

Students will learn that energy, strong feelings, and vivid details contribute to voice.

Materials

Student Rubric for Voice (Teacher's Guide page 41)
Sample Paper 11: Miss Obnoxious (Teacher's Guide page 152 and/or Overhead 11)

Scoring the Paper

1. Distribute copies of the sample paper and the Student Rubric for Voice. Use the rubric to focus students' attention on the key features of the trait of VOICE—energy, emotion, individuality, and the writer's interest in the topic and audience.
2. Have students think about these questions as they listen to you read the paper: *Is it fun to read aloud and to listen to? Would you share this paper with a friend? Does the writer seem engaged with the topic or bored? Do details contribute to voice?*
3. Ask students to score the paper individually, using the student rubric. They should mark their scores in writing, putting an **X** in the appropriate blank. (If students do not have copies of the sample paper, they can write on separate sheets of paper.)
4. Ask students to compare their responses with those of a partner. They should take a few minutes to talk about the paper and ask each other questions.
5. After three or four minutes, ask students to share their reasons for scoring the paper as they did.

Discussing the Paper

Discuss the paper with the class. Ask students to say what scores they gave the paper and why. The *why* is the most important part in deepening their understanding. Use the following questions to encourage discussion:

- Do you think you could recognize this writer's voice in another piece of writing? Why? Can you describe the voice in a word or two? What words would you choose?
- Were there places where the voice was especially strong? Where?
- Can you make a connection between vivid details and voice? Which details—if any—make this voice stronger? Why?
- Is this writer having a good time writing about his sister? How do you know?

*Rationale for the Score**

Most students should see this paper as **strong.** It received a **6,** based on the 6-point rubric. It has humor, energy, individuality, and is fun to read, whether silently or aloud. In many places, good use of detail helps make the voice strong. The closing is understated and maintains the humor. This writer paints a vivid portrait of himself as a victim. Notice the use of dialogue, which also contributes to voice.

Extensions

1. What if one or more of these events were told from Kristen's point of view? What would she have to say? Ask students to rewrite "Miss Obnoxious" from Kristen's point of view as a way of exploring another voice.
2. Ask students to create a dialogue between the two main characters, using one of the situations from the paper or an invented situation.
3. Have students brainstorm a list of words to describe the voice in "Miss Obnoxious."

*See Teacher's Guide page 195 for a 5-point rubric and page 208 for the score based on that rubric.

name: .... date: ....

Sample Paper 11: VOICE

Miss Obnoxious

If there were an award for "Most Obnoxious Sister," my sister would win. One of the worst things about my sister, Kristen, is that she thinks she is so smart because she gets As all of the time. She could turn in a blank piece of paper with a sticker in the middle, and it would be called "insightful art." If I turned in the same thing, I'd get the usual response: "You need to make a serious effort."

She can be mean, too. She pinches me when we're sitting next to each other in the car. She says it's because I am invading her space. And when she pinches me, I scream. Then my dad says to me, "Quiet! I'm trying to watch the traffic here." Pinching must be OK in our family, but screaming in agony is a violation of our family code of silence during traffic hours.

I dread when we get ready to go somewhere because she spends too much time in the bathroom. Meanwhile, I'm allowed three minutes to shower and brush my teeth so I won't make us late. "You're going to have to get faster," my mom told me. I did. I got so fast I beat Kristen into the bathroom the next day.

On the bright side, I suppose I have benefited from my experiences with Kristen. I no longer scream when I'm in pain, and I can brush my teeth in less than one minute. Most of all, I have learned to appreciate everyone else.

Mark the score that this paper should receive in the trait of VOICE. Read your rubric for Voice to help you decide.

___ 1 ___ 2 ___ 3 ___ 4 ___ 5 ___ 6

Sample Paper 12: Tornado

Objectives

Students will learn that even when a topic has potential, voice can falter when a writer tells about his or her feelings but does not share them.

Materials

Student Rubric for Voice (Teacher's Guide page 41)
Sample Paper 12: Tornado (Teacher's Guide page 155 and/or Overhead 12)

Scoring the Paper

1. Distribute copies of the sample paper and the Student Rubric for Voice. Use the rubric to focus students' attention on the key features of the trait of VOICE—energy, emotion, individuality, and the writer's interest in the topic and audience.
2. Have students think about these questions as they listen to you read the paper: *Is the paper lively? Is it fun to read aloud and to listen to? Would you share this paper with a friend? Is the paper personal, honest, and insightful?*
3. Ask students to score the paper individually, using the student rubric. They should mark their scores in writing, putting an **X** in the appropriate blank. (If students do not have copies of the sample paper, they can write on separate sheets of paper.)
4. Ask students to compare their responses with those of a partner. They should take a few minutes to talk about the paper and ask each other questions. Expect this process to be slow at first; they will talk more and come to agreement faster over time.
5. After three or four minutes, ask students to share their reasons for scoring the paper as they did.

Discussing the Paper

Discuss the paper with the class. Ask students to say what scores they gave the paper and why. The *why* is the most important part in deepening their understanding. Use the following questions to encourage discussion:

- How does the writer feel about tornadoes? Does he or she have strong feelings?
- Does the writer give us insight about those feelings? Do you share them? Why or why not?
- Would you want this paper to go on for several more pages? Why or why not?
- Would you read this paper aloud to a friend? Why or why not?

*Rationale for the Score**

Most students should see this paper as **in process.** It received a score of **2,** based on the 6-point rubric. The voice is not strong. (The writer sounds more like the calm before the storm rather than the storm itself!) The writer makes casual observations about the events that occurred but conveys no sense of urgency or panic—or even much concern, for that matter. This account has little energy—readers must wonder whether the writer truly was frightened by this experience.

Extensions

1. Brainstorm some things that people might feel or do in a truly frightening situation. How many of these details appear in "Tornado"? Ask students to use these details and revise the lead for this piece, creating the sense of fear someone in this situation might experience.
2. Ask students whether they can think of three things a writer could do to create a particular mood. Then ask each student to revise one scene in this piece by using one or more of these strategies.
3. Have student partners research tornadoes. Tell them to collect facts and other interesting information. Then have them use this knowledge of tornadoes to revise the paper and see the impact "insider" information has on voice. Discuss the difference it makes?

*See Teacher's Guide page 195 for a 5-point rubric and page 209 for the score based on that rubric.

name: .... date: ....

Sample Paper 12: VOICE

Tornado

Tornadoes can be really scary. The scariest experience I have ever had in my life was with a tornado. It happened last summer when I was visiting my grandmother's ranch in Texas. She lives near Dallas. Her house is not very big, but there are a lot of trees around it, and she has two big dogs, Trouble and Zinger. The tornado happened near her ranch. We could hear it coming. It was quite loud. We had heard a weather forecast that morning that said we might get thunderstorms, but they did not mention a tornado. At first it was calm and then the wind blew really hard. My grandfather made us go into the basement to be safe. Trouble and Zinger came, too. I figured if we had to go into the basement, there was probably something to be scared about. We couldn't have lights because the electricity went out. We were without electricity for about three or four hours. We had a radio with batteries, so we listened to the news because we wanted to know when it was safe to go back upstairs again. We didn't take any food with us because there wasn't time, and we all got pretty hungry, even the dogs. We could hear the storm outside the whole time we were in the basement. The house was not hurt or anything, but that was still my scariest experience. I still visit my grandparents, but that was the only time we had a tornado.

Mark the score that this paper should receive in the trait of VOICE.
Read your rubric for Voice to help you decide.

____ 1 ____ 2 ____ 3 ____ 4 ____ 5 ____ 6

Sample Paper 13: Mature Audiences Only

Objectives

Students will learn that word choice is enhanced by precise words and strong verbs.

Materials

Student Rubric for Word Choice (Teacher's Guide page 59)
Sample Paper 13: Mature Audiences Only (Teacher's Guide page 158 and/or Overhead 13)

Scoring the Paper

1. Distribute copies of the sample paper and the Student Rubric for Word Choice. Use the rubric to focus students' attention on the key features of the trait of WORD CHOICE—strong verbs, sensory language used correctly, and fresh, original use of everyday words.
2. Have students think about these questions as they listen to you read the paper: *Are the words clear? Does the writer use strong verbs? Are some words or phrases examples of strong word choice?*
3. Ask students to score the paper individually, using the student rubric. They should mark their scores in writing, putting an **X** in the appropriate blank. (If students do not have copies of the sample paper, they can write on separate sheets of paper.)
4. Ask students to compare their responses with those of a partner. They should take a few minutes to talk about the paper and ask each other questions.
5. After three or four minutes, ask students to share their reasons for scoring the paper as they did.

Discussing the Paper

Discuss the paper with the class. Ask students to say what scores they gave the paper and why. The *why* is the most important part in deepening their understanding. Use the following questions to encourage discussion:

- Do you have favorite words or phrases in this paper? Identify them.
- Should any words be replaced? Identify them. Can you think of some better word choices?
- Are word meanings always clear from the way the writer uses them?

*Rationale for the Score**

Most students should see this paper as **strong.** It received a score of **6,** based on the 6-point rubric. Though "Mature Audiences Only" will not send readers scrambling for the dictionary, it does contain some fresh, original use of everyday language: *we'd develop a preference for thought-provoking entertainment.* In addition, the piece is peppered generously with strong verbs: *wonder, express,* and *squeezing.* Strong word choice clarifies meaning and enhances voice, which in this paper seems self-assured and informed. The writing is not wordy and repetitive, nor is it overwritten.

Extensions

1. Did your students mark any words or phrases be replaced? If so, brainstorm some possible alternatives and discuss them. Would they improve the paper?
2. How do your students characterize this writer's use of language? Is it impressive—or just everyday language used thoughtfully? Discuss their responses.
3. Do your students agree with this writer's point of view? Does the writer present a convincing case? Invite students to write a response to this paper, either voicing support or raising a contrary point of view. Remind them to attend closely to word choice as they write.

*See Teacher's Guide page 196 for a 5-point rubric and page 209 for the score based on that rubric.

name: .... date: ....

Sample Paper 13: WORD CHOICE

Mature Audiences Only

When I see those announcements that say, "Warning: This program is for mature audiences only," I always wonder what on earth they are thinking. Is language that is unacceptable for me to use OK for adults?

We are told that certain programs contain "adult language." Aren't adults supposed to express themselves in a mature, socially acceptable way? That's what my parents tell me, but apparently they've got it wrong. I guess squeezing every conceivable obscenity into each sentence is a measure of maturity.

If we were truly mature, maybe we'd develop a preference for thought-provoking entertainment. We would want to hear respectful language used well—at least most of the time. I think we need to hear more from writers, filmmakers, and even newscasters who wish to educate us. Must TV programs always broadcast horrifying, dangerous, and depressing stories? Every now and then we might be interested in a person tutoring nonreaders or providing medical aid or discovering a breakthrough way to make food and water safe. Then we could announce before the news, "For mature audiences only" and really mean it.

Mark the score that this paper should receive in the trait of WORD CHOICE. Read your rubric for Word Choice to help you decide.

____ 1 ____ 2 ____ 3 ____ 4 ____ 5 ____ 6

Sample Paper 14: Having Braces

Objectives

Students will learn that weak word choice can produce vague and repetitive language.

Materials

Student Rubric for Word Choice (Teacher's Guide page 59)
Sample Paper 14: Having Braces (Teacher's Guide page 161 and/or Overhead 14)

Scoring the Paper

1. Distribute copies of the sample paper and the Student Rubric for Word Choice. Use the rubric to focus students' attention on the key features of the trait of WORD CHOICE—strong verbs, sensory language used correctly, and fresh, original use of everyday words.
2. Have students think about these questions as they listen to you read the paper: *Does the writer use any especially effective words or phrases? Are any words vague, overdone, or repeated too often?*
3. Ask students to score the paper individually, using the student rubric. They should mark their scores in writing, putting an **X** in the appropriate blank. (If students do not have copies of the sample paper, they can write on separate sheets of paper.)
4. Ask students to compare their responses with those of a partner. They should take a few minutes to talk about the paper and ask each other questions.
5. After three or four minutes, ask students to share their reasons for scoring the paper as they did.

Discussing the Paper

Discuss the paper with the class. Ask students to say what scores they gave the paper and why. The *why* is the most important part in deepening their understanding. Use the following questions to encourage discussion:

- Do you have any favorite words or phrases in this paper? Which ones?
- Does this writer use strong verbs?
- Are any words overused? Which ones?
- Do the words paint a clear picture in your mind?

*Rationale for the Score**

Most students should see this paper as **in process.** It received a **3,** based on the 6-point rubric. Though the basic meaning is reasonably clear, the paper needs stronger verbs and more vivid, precise language. Many words are repeated, making the writing cluttered and imprecise. Nearly every reader knows something about the experience of getting braces. Readers need more precise and interesting word choices that provide a new perspective or personal impression.

Extensions

1. With your students, brainstorm a collection of words, phrases, and sensory impressions that relate to the experience of getting braces. Put these on an overhead. Ask students to use this word cache to create a revised paragraph that makes the whole experience more vivid.
2. Discuss how word choice influences voice in "Having Braces," and then score the piece for voice as a class. Chances are, your students will score it somewhere along the low end to midpoint of the scale. It is difficult to achieve strong voice when the language is flat.
3. This writer uses numerous exclamation points. Discuss with students whether exclamation points can take the place of strong words. Then have students imagine that they are interviewers who will discuss this issue with the exclamation point (as if it were a real person). Tell them to write this discussion as a short dialogue, writing about word choice and voice from the exclamation point's view.

*See Teacher's Guide page 196 for a 5-point rubric and page 209 for the score based on that rubric.

name: .... date: ....

Sample Paper 14: WORD CHOICE

Having Braces

Having braces is not a great experience. It is really, really unfair that my brother gets away with not having braces at all, and I have to have braces. The dentist says I need to wear the braces for at least two years! Two years is a really, really long time! Every few weeks (this is the really bad part) I have to go to see the dentist and have my braces tightened. When I have them tightened, it hurts. It is not really that bad, but it is bad enough! It hurts enough so that it is hard not to think about it. I never feel like eating or talking. Right after I have my braces tightened, I have a hard time concentrating on my homework, and I do not feel like smiling!!! My parents tell me that I will be really thankful that I had braces after my teeth are nice and straight. I am sure they are right, but I wish my teeth were nice and straight right now. Then I would not need braces at all.

Mark the score that this paper should receive in the trait of WORD CHOICE. Read your rubric for Word Choice to help you decide. Then write your reason for the score.

___ 1 ___ 2 ___ 3 ___ 4 ___ 5 ___ 6

____

____

Sample Paper 15: Planting Tomatoes

Objectives

Students will learn that choosing the right words for the intended meaning creates strong voice.

Materials

Student Rubric for Word Choice (Teacher's Guide page 59)
Sample Paper 15: Planting Tomatoes (Teacher's Guide page 164 and/or Overhead 15)

Scoring the Paper

1. Distribute copies of the sample paper and the Student Rubric for Word Choice. Use the rubric to focus students' attention on the key features of the trait of WORD CHOICE—strong verbs, sensory language used correctly, and fresh, original use of everyday words.
2. Have students think about these questions as they listen to you read the paper: *Does the writer use any strong verbs or sensory language? Are any words or phrases especially effective? Are any words unnecessary or overused?*
3. Ask students to score the paper individually, using the student rubric. They should mark their scores in writing, putting an **X** in the appropriate blank. (If students do not have copies of the sample paper, they can write on separate sheets of paper.)
4. Ask students to compare their responses with those of a partner. They should take a few minutes to talk about the paper and ask each other questions.
5. After three or four minutes, ask students to share their reasons for scoring the paper as they did.

Discussing the Paper

Discuss the paper with the class. Ask students to say what scores they gave the paper and why. The *why* is the most important part in deepening their understanding. Use the following questions to encourage discussion:

- Do you have any favorite words or phrases in this paper?
- Do all the words make sense as the writer uses them? Which ones do not?
- Do you notice any strong verbs? Name some.
- Are any words used too often? If so, which ones?
- Do the words paint a clear picture in your mind? How? Is the picture vivid enough to turn into a film? Why?

*Rationale for the Score**

Most students should see this paper as **in process.** It received a **2,** based on the 6-point rubric, because the piece is filled with overwritten phrases that simply do not work. These may have come from the writer's imagination, but they seem to be evidence of thesaurus overuse: *the enterprise of planting tomatoes with euphoria and zest, the most prestigious tomatoes, a vivacious tomato plant, implant the tomato,* and so on. The result is a hard-to-read piece on a simple topic: How to plant a tomato. This lofty language is overkill with such a simple subject, which is why readers might be distracted from the message.

Extensions

1. This writer of "Planting Tomatoes" seems to have relied too much on a thesaurus. What if a thesaurus came with a warning label? What might that label say? Invite your students to write text for a good thesaurus warning label.
2. This paper seems to have one standout problem: overwritten language (thesaurus overuse syndrome). Ask students to check their own writing for this common pitfall. They should revise based on any problems they see.
3. Assign each unfamiliar word from "Planting Tomatoes" to an "expert," who will look up the meaning or possible meanings in a dictionary. Then reread the paper, and have these experts help interpret. Now what do students think of the word choice? Does it make sense?

*See Teacher's Guide page 196 for a 5-point rubric and page 210 for the score based on that rubric.

name: .... date: ....

Sample Paper 15: Word Choice

Planting Tomatoes

Most gardeners approach the enterprise of planting tomatoes with euphoria and zest. A few simple things can facilitate you to grow the most prestigious tomatoes you can grow. The first thing to do is choose a vivacious tomato plant. It should be healthy, with luxuriant green leaves and a robust and powerful stem. When you implant the tomato, dig a pretty big hole and inject some mulch. Add water also. Insert the deciduous tomato into the hole, and be sure to thrust it deep into the ground, working partially up the length of your arm. Promulgate additional mulch to envelop the roots and even part of the stem. Then amplify the mulch and water as required. Be sure to situate the tomato in a sunny spot. Tomatoes reflect a strong preference for full sun. Give the tomato some fertilizer, but exercise caution. If you give it too much, the tomato plant itself will burgeon, but will not stimulate many tomatoes. Continue watering the tomato plant the whole duration of the time it is growing. Increase the water when actual tomatoes become recognizable on the plant. Now you know all the secrets of growing exemplary tomatoes.

Mark the score that this paper should receive in the trait of WORD CHOICE. Read your rubric for Word Choice to help you decide. Then write your reason for the score.

____ 1 ____ 2 ____ 3 ____ 4 ____ 5 ____ 6

____

____

Sample Paper 16: Go with the Flow!

Objectives

Students will learn that strong, active phrases and powerful verbs can enhance word choice.

Materials

Student Rubric for Word Choice (Teacher's Guide page 59)
Sample Paper 16: Go with the Flow! (Teacher's Guide page 167 and/or Overhead 16)

Scoring the Paper

1. Distribute copies of the sample paper and the Student Rubric for Word Choice. Use the rubric to focus students' attention on the key features of the trait of WORD CHOICE—strong verbs, sensory language that is not overdone, and fresh, original use of everyday words.
2. Have students think about these questions as they listen to you read the paper: *Does the writer use strong verbs or sensory language? Are any words or phrases especially effective?*
3. Ask students to score the paper individually, using the student rubric. They should mark their scores in writing, putting an **X** in the appropriate blank. (If students do not have copies of the sample paper, they can write on separate sheets of paper.)
4. Ask students to compare their responses with those of a partner. They should take a few minutes to talk about the paper and ask each other questions.
5. After three or four minutes, ask students to share their reasons for scoring the paper as they did.

Discussing the Paper

Discuss the paper with the class. Ask students to say what scores they gave the paper and why. The *why* is the most important part in deepening their understanding. Use the following questions to encourage discussion:

- Did you find any strong words or phrases in this piece? Identify them.
- Are there any places where you would have used words differently. If so, where?
- Does the writer use sensory words or details? If so, where?
- Is the language vivid enough to put you at the scene?

*Rationale for the Score**

Most students should see this paper as **fairly strong.** It received a **4,** based on the 6-point rubric. The language is clear and refreshing, like the river ride itself, and contains some strong moments: *smooth and tranquil; foamy water; we were drenched; slippery, silky waters; spinning like a giant Frisbee;* and *conquered.* Some of the language is a bit predictable: *our aching arms* and *we were all smiles.* These expressions are clear and help provide a picture of the raft going down the rapids. Yet the writer might have stretched a bit harder to provide original phrasing and details for someone who hasn't experienced river rafting. On the other hand, the words are never confusing or overwritten.

Extensions

1. Try a group write-around in which each paragraph is assigned to a different group for a quick shot-in-the-arm revision. Groups can change words slightly, add a phrase, or take something out to give the piece more energy. Have groups read their revised paragraphs in the order in which they appear in the paper. What differences do students detect?
2. The writer uses a few strong verbs but might have used many more had he or she focused on the movements of the river and the rafters. Ask students, in small groups, to brainstorm a list of "action moments" that capture the movements of the river and the rafters. Then, choosing their favorites, they should arrange these in any order they like to create a poem on rafting. Remind them to give each poem a title. Read the poems aloud, and share one you have written with one of the groups.

*See Teacher's Guide page 196 for a 5-point rubric and page 210 for the score based on that rubric.

name: .... date: ....

Sample Paper 16: WORD CHOICE

Go with the Flow!

When I first heard that our family was going rafting on the Colorado River, I got chills. Maybe it was anticipation or just fear. I'm still not sure which!

From that first tumble down the easiest rapids, I knew river rafting would be my new passion. At first, though, the river was smooth and tranquil. Within minutes, though, we were drenched. We could hear the rapids churning as we approached. Then, swoosh! Our raft slid over the foamy water and spun around as we laughed like kids on a giant water slide.

Throughout the daylong journey, we glided through slippery, silky waters and lurched through hold-on-for-dear-life rapids. We worked hard to keep our raft upright and centered. It was a challenge that demanded every bit of strength our aching arms could muster. The river was stronger than we were and seemed to know it. Several times it sent our raft spinning like a giant Frisbee.

When we cleared the last rapids and floated onto the smooth homestretch, we were all smiles because we had done it! We had conquered our fear—at least for that ride!

Mark the score that this paper should receive in the trait of WORD CHOICE. Read your rubric for Word Choice to help you decide.

____ 1 ____ 2 ____ 3 ____ 4 ____ 5 ____ 6

Sample Paper 17: Mosquitoes, Beware!

Objectives

Students will learn that writing is monotonous when it is filled with choppy, repetitive sentences or sentences that begin in identical or similar ways.

Materials

Student Rubric for Sentence Fluency (Teacher's Guide page 77)
Sample Paper 17: Mosquitoes, Beware! (Teacher's Guide page 170 and/or Overhead 17)

Scoring the Paper

1. Distribute copies of the sample paper and the Student Rubric for Sentence Fluency. Use the rubric to focus students' attention on the key features of SENTENCE FLUENCY—students should look and listen for differences in sentence beginnings and sentence lengths, run-ons or rambling sentences, natural dialogue, and a smooth flow of ideas.
2. Have students think about these questions as they listen to you read the paper: *Is this paper easy to read aloud? Do sentences vary in length? Are sentence beginnings varied and purposeful?*
3. Ask students to score the paper individually, using the student rubric. They should mark their scores in writing, putting an **X** in the appropriate blank. (If students do not have copies of the sample paper, they can write on separate sheets of paper.)
4. Ask students to compare their responses with those of a partner. They should take a few minutes to talk about the paper and ask each other questions.
5. After three or four minutes, ask students to share their reasons for scoring the paper as they did.

Discussing the Paper

Discuss the paper with the class. Ask students to say what scores they gave the paper and why. The *why* is the most important part in deepening their understanding. Use the following questions to encourage discussion:

- Does the writing sound smooth or choppy? Explain.
- Do many sentences begin in different ways? Are specific sentence beginnings repeated? Which ones?
- Do the sentences vary in length, or are most about the same length?
- Is it difficult to read this paper aloud? Do you need to practice? Why?

*Rationale for the Score**

Most students should see this paper as still **in process.** It received a **3,** based on the 6-point rubric (some students may see it as a 2), because it is extremely choppy and so difficult to read with inflection. The sentences are nearly all the same length. Further, many sentences begin with the words *this, if,* or *it.* Though the word *mosquitoes* is not often used as a sentence starter, it is repeated so many times that the repetition disrupts the fluency. In addition, sentence beginnings provide virtually no link between ideas; the writer does not make use of transitional phrases, such as *in the meantime* and *on the other hand.* On the positive side, the writer uses complete sentences and has included no run-ons.

Extensions

1. Ask students to practice reading a piece of their own writing aloud. What sentence fluency problems do they encounter? This is a good time for some revision!
2. "Mosquitoes, Beware!" is a good paper to use for practicing sentence combining. Ask students to work in pairs. Remind them that it is not necessary to combine every sentence. If an idea has been stated, it need not be repeated. Also remind students to use transitional phrases to clarify the connections between sentences or ideas. Be sure to read revisions aloud.
3. Have students rewrite the piece as advertising copy for Ace Mosquito Repellent, pretending that this copy will be read aloud on TV or on the radio. Have several students present their ads accompanied by background music. Comment on the fluency.

*See Teacher's Guide page 197 for a 5-point rubric and page 211 for the score based on that rubric.

name: .... date: ....

Sample Paper 17: SENTENCE FLUENCY

Mosquitoes, Beware!

A new kind of mosquito repellent is coming. This new repellent is made from tomatoes. That's right, tomatoes. It turns out mosquitoes hate tomatoes. So some scientists used tomatoes to make a mosquito repellent. It really works, too. It works better than you might think. It also is not as harmful to humans as chemical repellents. It has no bad side effects. It just keeps the mosquitoes away. Mosquitoes are terrible pests that carry disease. If we have a harmless way to get rid of mosquitoes, we should use it. If this kind of repellent works, maybe scientists will develop other products that use tomatoes. If they can use tomatoes, maybe other vegetables will work as well. Maybe we should plant more tomatoes in our yards! This could make sitting outside a lot more pleasant. You might be wondering if you could just rub tomato juice on yourself. This would save buying an expensive repellent. It sounds like a good idea. Scientists say this does not work, however. However, it won't hurt you!

Mark the score that this paper should receive in the trait of SENTENCE FLUENCY. Read your rubric for Sentence Fluency to help you decide. Then write your reason for the score.

____ 1 ____ 2 ____ 3 ____ 4 ____ 5 ____ 6

____

____

Sample Paper 18: Hold the Garlic, Please!

Objectives

Students will learn that writing is fluent and readable when sentences vary in both length and structure.

Materials

Student Rubric for Sentence Fluency (Teacher's Guide page 77)
Sample Paper 18: Hold the Garlic, Please! (Teacher's Guide page 173 and/or Overhead 18)

Scoring the Paper

1. Distribute copies of the sample paper and the Student Rubric for Sentence Fluency. Use the rubric to focus students' attention on the key features of SENTENCE FLUENCY. Students should look and listen for differences in sentence beginnings and sentence lengths, run-ons or rambling sentences, natural dialogue, and a smooth flow of ideas.
2. Have students think about these questions as they listen to you read the paper: *Is this paper easy to read aloud—and easy on the ear, too? Do sentences vary in length? Are sentence beginnings varied and purposeful?*
3. Ask students to score the paper individually, using the student rubric. They should mark their scores in writing, putting an **X** in the appropriate blank. (If students do not have copies of the sample paper, they can write on separate sheets of paper.)
4. Ask students to compare their responses with those of a partner. They should take a few minutes to talk about the paper and ask each other questions.
5. After three or four minutes, ask students to share their reasons for scoring the paper as they did.

Discussing the Paper

Discuss the paper with the class. Ask students to say what scores they gave the paper and why. The *why* is the most important part in deepening their understanding. Use the following questions to encourage discussion:

- Did the writing sound smooth or choppy? Explain.
- Did you hear and see a lot of variety in sentence lengths? How about sentence beginnings—a lot of variety or only a little?
- Does this paper seem difficult or easy to read? Explain.
- This writer uses some fragments. Does this help or hinder fluency? Why?

*Rationale for the Score**

Most students should see this paper as **strong.** We gave it a **6,** based on the 6-point rubric. The sentences vary in both length and structure. The shortest is only three words long and the longest contains twenty-nine words. Students should not become too formulaic or statistical in their analysis of writing, but this count verifies the extent of variety in this piece. Virtually every sentence begins in a slightly different way (compare Sample Paper 17). Reading the paper aloud expressively helps bring out voice.

Extensions

1. Read aloud the first few words of every sentence in "Hold the Garlic, Please!" What do students notice? Now, ask each student to review a piece of his or her own writing and do this same exercise. Do they hear fluency or the need for revision?

2. Have students rewrite "Hold the Garlic, Please!" as a free-verse poem—perhaps an "Ode to Garlic." Students may vary the length of lines, take out words, add dialogue, and use fragments, and repetition, but they may not change the topic. Read results aloud. Talk about the fluency that can be achieved with poetry.

3. What if the author of Paper 17 ("Mosquitoes, Beware!") had written "Hold the Garlic, Please!" How would it sound? Ask students to rewrite "Hold the Garlic, Please!" in the style of "Mosquitoes, Beware!" You can divide the work into sections (by paragraph) if you wish, and students can work with partners. Then, read the results aloud followed by a volunteer's reading of the original "Hold the Garlic, Please!" Discuss the differences you hear and how much voice this "revised" version loses.

*See Teacher's Guide page 197 for a 5-point rubric and page 211 for the score based on that rubric.

name: .... date: ....

Sample Paper 18: SENTENCE FLUENCY

Hold the Garlic, Please!

Is it really necessary to include garlic in everything? This is America, of course. So you should be able to eat garlic at every meal if you wish, right? What about the rights of non-garlic lovers, though? Garlic is served to me—uninvited—in everything from spices to mashed potatoes to Caesar salad. It's even in ice cream! What's more, those of us who prefer not to indulge must breathe in secondhand garlic if we talk to those who have indulged. Mouthwash is of no help. Brushing doesn't help either. As soon as you consume it, garlic consumes you, oozing from every pore and vaporizing to form a protective yet invisible cloud that only other garlic lovers can penetrate.

I'll be honest. For several years, I've been working to change my tastes. After all, since garlic is so popular, I might as well learn to like it, right? Sorry, garlic fans, but I don't think it's going to happen. Many years and countless breath mints later, I am no closer to enjoying garlic-flavored chips, noodles—or friends. Still, I don't suppose garlic fans want to give up the pleasures of the clove either. How about a compromise? It's all I ask. Wouldn't that be refreshing?

Mark the score that this paper should receive in the trait of SENTENCE FLUENCY. Read your rubric for Sentence Fluency to help you decide.

____ 1 ____ 2 ____ 3 ____ 4 ____ 5 ____ 6

Sample Paper 19: It's for You

Objectives

Students will learn that dialogue, if it is well done and sounds natural, adds to the fluency of a piece of writing.

Materials

Student Rubric for Sentence Fluency (Teacher's Guide page 77)
Sample Paper 19: It's for You (Teacher's Guide page 176 and/or Overhead 19)

Scoring the Paper

1. Distribute copies of the sample paper and the Student Rubric for Sentence Fluency. Use the rubric to focus students' attention on the key features of the trait of SENTENCE FLUENCY. Students should look and listen for differences in sentence beginnings and sentence lengths, run-ons or rambling sentences, natural dialogue, and a smooth flow of ideas.
2. Have students think about these questions as they listen to you read the paper: *Is this paper easy to read aloud—and easy on the ear, too? Do sentences vary in length? Do you hear or see any run-on sentences? Does the dialogue sound natural?*
3. Ask students to score the paper individually, using the student rubric. They should mark their scores in writing, putting an **X** in the appropriate blank. (If students do not have copies of the sample paper, they can write on separate sheets of paper.)
4. Ask students to compare their responses with those of a partner. They should take a few minutes to talk about the paper and ask each other questions.
5. After three or four minutes, ask students to share their reasons for scoring the paper as they did.

Discussing the Paper

Discuss the paper with the class. Ask students to say what scores they gave the paper and why. The *why* is the most important part in deepening their understanding. Use the following questions to encourage discussion:

- Did the writing sound smooth? Explain.
- Did you hear or see any run-on sentences? If so, where?
- Does this paper seem difficult or easy to read? Explain.
- Does the dialogue sound like real speech? Explain.

*Rationale for the Score**

Most students should see this paper as **strong.** It received a **5,** based on the 6-point rubric, because it is varied in structure and sentence length and is easy to read. In addition, the dialogue is natural and works well. It only misses receiving a score of 6 because many sentences begin with *we, he,* or *I*—and it does not have the variety in sentence length of Sample Paper 18 ("Hold the Garlic, Please!").

Extensions

1. For a challenge: Invite students to write the entire story in dialogue. Can they do it? Try it yourself—it isn't as easy as you might think! Read the results aloud. What are the challenges of writing dialogue?
2. Have students revise the piece so that no sentences begin with the words *I, We, He, It, The,* and *This.* Read the result aloud to hear the difference this change makes?
3. Ask each student to review a sample of his or her own writing and to examine sentence beginnings. Have them revise, as necessary, to vary sentence beginnings.
4. Have students score the paper for organization (scores should be fairly high). The writer waits until the end to reveal the truth about the starling mimicking the sound of the phone ringing. Do students think this is a good idea, or do they think that the writer should state this sooner? Have them explain their responses.

*See Teacher's Guide page 197 for a 5-point rubric and page 211 for the score based on that rubric.

name: .... date: ....

Sample Paper 19: SENTENCE FLUENCY

It's for You

"The phone's ringing," my father said, never looking up from his work on our deck. I heard another ring followed by his voice again.

"Hey, somebody get the phone. I think it's the cell phone."

"Dad, the phone isn't ringing," I replied as I continued fixing myself a sandwich. He looked up, just as we heard another ring. We stared at each other, wondering what to make of it. Clearly, someone's phone was ringing; but it wasn't ours, and we couldn't see a person or a cell phone anywhere. "Well, what in blazes . . . ," my dad started to say.

Just then, a starling flew from a branch just over Dad's head. The bird was "ringing" as it flew away. "Dad," I laughed, "It's for you!" He had to laugh, too.

We had just discovered what scientists have known for years—that starlings can mimic almost any kind of sound, including the sound of a cell phone. Next time you think your telephone is ringing, you might want to first check the nearest tree branch. The call might not be for you after all.

Mark the score that this paper should receive in the trait of SENTENCE FLUENCY. Read your rubric for Sentence Fluency to help you decide.

____ 1 ____ 2 ____ 3 ____ 4 ____ 5 ____ 6

Sample Paper 20: Moving

Objectives

Students will learn that run-on sentences or sentences joined with endless connectives can get in the way of fluency.

Materials

Student Rubric for Sentence Fluency (Teacher's Guide page 77)
Sample Paper 20: Moving (Teacher's Guide page 179 and/or Overhead 20)

Scoring the Paper

1. Distribute copies of the sample paper and the Student Rubric for Sentence Fluency. Use the rubric to focus students' attention on the key features of the trait of SENTENCE FLUENCY. Students should look and listen for differences in sentence beginnings and sentence lengths, run-ons or rambling sentences, natural dialogue, and a smooth flow of ideas.
2. Have students think about these questions as they listen to you read the paper: *Is this paper easy to read aloud—and easy on the ear, too? Do sentences vary in length? Are there any run-on sentences? Does the writer use too many connecting words (and, so, because, but, so on)?*
3. Ask students to score the paper individually, using the student rubric. They should mark their scores in writing, putting an **X** in the appropriate blank. (If students do not have copies of the sample paper, they can write on separate sheets of paper.)
4. Ask students to compare their responses with those of a partner. They should take a few minutes to talk about the paper and ask each other questions.
5. After three or four minutes, ask students to share their reasons for scoring the paper as they did.

Discussing the Paper

Discuss the paper with the class. Ask students to say what scores they gave the paper and why. The *why* is the most important part in deepening their understanding. Use the following questions to encourage discussion:

- Did the writing sound smooth? Is the paper easy to read aloud?
- Did you hear or see any run-on sentences? If so, where?
- Notice the connecting words. Does the writer use enough of these? Too many? Or is it about right?

*Rationale for the Score**

Most students should see this paper as **in process.** It received a **2,** based on the 6-point rubric, because it is quite difficult to read aloud. Some sentences are run-ons and clearly need to be separated. Others, though, are joined by connecting words, such as *and,* and are much too long. Extra words should be crossed out, extra connectives eliminated, and run-ons repaired.

Extensions

1. Ask a volunteer to read this aloud (or split the task between two students). Ask readers to comment on the fluency.
2. Ask students to work with a partner and revise "Moving." They should feel free to cross out words, add punctuation, or do whatever is necessary to improve fluency. Have them compare the fluency in both versions.
3. Tell students that some people believe that leaving out some punctuation and hooking together multiple sentences captures natural speech patterns. Do students agree or disagree? Have a debate about this. Ask students to argue the point that writing should differ from speech. Is there a place for this kind of writing? Where?

*See Teacher's Guide page 197 for a 5-point rubric and page 212 for the score based on that rubric.

name: .... date: ....

Sample Paper 20: Sentence Fluency

Moving

We were barely settled in California when my dad got transferred to another location and so we had to move and I did not like it one bit. The thing about moving, well there's a million things, but one thing about moving is you have to pack and that means everything you own, right down to the tiniest things like pencils and paper clips and bathroom tissue and underwear and socks.

On top of everything else I had to leave my two best friends we had only known each other for two years but it seemed like we had been friends all our lives and leaving them was the pits. The other thing that really bothered me is that we were moving to a totally different place where we had never even visited namely Iowa which is pretty different from California and it is different in other ways too. And I have only been here for two months and besides that, I do not have one single really good friend in school yet I do not know if I will ever in a million years get used to it besides that it makes me crazy having parents who like to move so much it is weird.

Mark the score that this paper should receive in the trait of SENTENCE FLUENCY. Read your rubric for Sentence Fluency to help you decide. Then write your reason for the score.

___ 1 ___ 2 ___ 3 ___ 4 ___ 5 ___ 6

____

____

Sample Paper 21: Handling Food Carefully

Objectives

Students will recognize that errors in conventions can slow a reader down or make the writer's message hard to understand.

Materials

Student Rubric for Conventions (Teacher's Guide page 95)
Sample Paper 21: Handling Food Carefully (Teacher's Guide page 182 and/or Overhead 21)

Scoring the Paper

1. Distribute copies of the sample paper and the Student Rubric for Conventions. Use the rubric to focus students' attention on the key features of the trait of CONVENTIONS. Students should look for missing or repeated words and any errors in spelling, punctuation, grammar, and capitalization.
2. Have students think about these questions as they read the paper: *Does the writer make just one or two kinds of errors—or many kinds of errors? Does the writer use conventions skillfully to make the text easy to process?*
3. Ask students to score the paper individually, using the student rubric. They should mark their scores in writing, putting an **X** in the appropriate blank. (If students do not have copies of the sample paper, they can write on separate sheets of paper.)
4. Ask students to compare their responses with those of a partner. They should take a few minutes to talk about the paper and ask each other questions.
5. After three or four minutes, ask students to share their reasons for scoring the paper as they did.

Discussing the Paper

Discuss the paper with the class. Ask students to say what scores they gave the paper and why. The *why* is the most important part in deepening their understanding. Use the following questions to encourage discussion:

- Do you find many errors in this writing? A few errors? No errors?
- Do errors slow you down or cause you to reread?
- Does this writer make a variety of errors or mainly one or two types of errors?
- How much editing would need to be done to prepare this paper for publication?

*Rationale for the Score**

Most students should see this paper as **in process.** It received a **2,** based on the 6-point rubric. Although it is possible to decipher the writer's message, the many errors in conventions slow a reader down. Further, there are many types of errors, including missing words, extra words, misspellings, omitted commas, extra commas, omitted capital letters, an omitted period, and omitted apostrophes. This text would need extensive editing to be ready for publication.

Extensions

1. Ask students to identify the errors and to mark them with appropriate editor's symbols. They should check with partners when they have finished.
2. Ask students to be editorial consultants for you and tell you how to mark the text as you work on the overhead. They should compare their edited text with the corrections you create as you go.
3. How much do the errors in this text interfere with ideas? Not at all? Slightly? Moderately? A lot? Take a vote, and ask students to write short paragraphs defending their votes. Have volunteers read paragraphs aloud. This is good practice for creating a persuasive essay.

*See Teacher's Guide page 198 for a 5-point rubric and page 212 for the score based on that rubric.

name: .... date: ....

Sample Paper 21: CONVENTIONS

Handling Food Carefully

You may have seen, a headline in the newpaper lately about another outbreak of the diseas known as salmonella poisoning. Salmonela bacteria lives everwhere and are on most of the foods we ate. If we do do not wash the food properly or cook meat thoroughly, we can get sick. It a good idea to wash all fruits and vegetables with soap or a special solution. You shold aslo wash your hands when handling food, of coarse, plus the surfaces food touches Its an exellent idea to have a meat thermomoter and to use it routinely when you are cooking roast beef, chicken, ham, or turkey. Many people like there steaks or burgers on the rare side, but cooking and eating them this way, is extreme dangerous. It can make. you very ill. another good way to get sick is to use a knife to slice meat for the oven or grill and then, without washing it, use that same nife to cut tomatoes lettuce, or other raw vegetables. People does this all the time and then wonder why they get sick. cook your food thorough, wash your hands, wash all dishes, counter surfaces and utensils, and the food itself, and you should have know problems?

Mark the score that this paper should receive in the trait of CONVENTIONS. Read your rubric for Conventions to help you decide. Then write your reason for the score.

____ 1 ____ 2 ____ 3 ____ 4 ____ 5 ____ 6

____

____

Sample Paper 22: Worms—They're Everywhere

Objectives

Students will recognize that noting and correcting even some errors makes text more readable.

Materials

Student Rubric for Conventions (Teacher's Guide page 95)
Sample Paper 22: Worms—They're Everywhere (Teacher's Guide page 185 and/or Overhead 22)

Scoring the Paper

1. Distribute copies of the sample paper and the Student Rubric for Conventions. Use the rubric to focus students' attention on the key features of the trait of CONVENTIONS. Students should look for missing or repeated words and any errors in spelling, punctuation, grammar, and capitalization.
2. Have students think about these questions as they read the paper: *Does this paper appear to be edited? Is this writer in control of conventions? Do any errors get in the way of readability?*
3. Ask students to score the paper individually, using the student rubric. They should mark their scores in writing, putting an **X** in the appropriate blank. (If students do not have copies of the sample paper, they can write on separate sheets of paper.)
4. Ask students to compare their responses with those of a partner. They should take a few minutes to talk about the paper and ask each other questions.
5. After three or four minutes, ask students to share their reasons for scoring the paper as they did.

Discussing the Paper

Discuss the paper with the class. Ask students to say what scores they gave the paper and why. The *why* is the most important part in deepening their understanding. Use the following questions to encourage discussion:

- Do you find many errors in this writing? A few errors? No errors at all?
- Do errors slow you down or cause you to reread?
- Does this writer's use of conventions make the paper easier or harder to read? How?
- How much editing would need to be done to prepare this paper for publication?

*Rationale for the Score**

Most students should see this paper as **fairly strong.** It received a **4,** based on the 6-point rubric. Although the paper does not have many errors, there are enough that a careful reader will notice them. On the other hand, errors do not seriously interfere with readability. This might be termed a "lightly edited" piece; another careful editing will prepare it for publication.

Extensions

1. Have students mark the errors on the sample paper. How many errors did students find? (They should have found 10 in all.) Did students find "errors" where none exist?
2. If students have questions about any of the conventions in this sample, refer to the *Write Source 2000* handbook. (See Teacher's Guide page 96.)
3. As a class, compile a list of things this writer does correctly. How long is that list? Compile a similar list of errors this writer commits. In balance, how is this writer doing?
4. Ask each student to review a piece of his or her writing and then make a two-column list. In the left column, have them list types of errors they each made. In the right column, have them list examples of what they each have done correctly. What is the balance? Ask student partners to compare and discuss results.

*See Teacher's Guide page 198 for a 5-point rubric and page 212 for the score based on that rubric.

name: .... date: ....

Sample Paper 22: CONVENTIONS

Worms—They're Everywhere

Ever watch a robin hoping around your yard and wonder whether it was finding any worms to eat? Chances are it was because an acer of fertile land can contain up to one million earthworms. Those worms help crops or any kind of plants to grow by aerating the soil. They eat tons of dead leaves and other plant parts in the course of a year and may move as much as 40 ton of soil during that time! Earthworms in africa can grow as long as 12 inches. One kind in Australia is almost 12 feet long. Imagine fishing with a worm that size!

Worms live almost anywhere, not just in the ground. Many worms live in the oceans. Some can tolerate high heat and live near underwater volcanoes. Worms is among the few creatures that can survive in Antarctica, where they can be found between sheets of ice. They also live, inside plants and other animals, including humans and many types of pets.

Scientists believe that worms have lived Earth for about half a billion years. no wonder they have adopted to life under so many condition.

Mark the score that this paper should receive in the trait of CONVENTIONS. Read your rubric for Conventions to help you decide.

___ 1 ___ 2 ___ 3 ___ 4 ___ 5 ___ 6

Sample Paper 23: Golf Mania

Objectives

Students will recognize that clean, well-edited text makes writing easy to read and understand.

Materials

Student Rubric for Conventions (Teacher's Guide page 95)
Sample Paper 23: Golf Mania (Teacher's Guide page 188 and/or Overhead 23)

Scoring the Paper

1. Distribute copies of the sample paper and the Student Rubric for Conventions. Use the rubric to focus students' attention on the key features of CONVENTIONS. Students should look for missing or repeated words and any errors in spelling, punctuation, grammar, and capitalization.
2. Have students think about these questions as they read the paper: *Does this paper appear to be edited? Is this writer in control of conventions? Do any errors get in the way of readability?*
3. Ask students to score the paper individually, using the student rubric. They should mark their scores in writing, putting an **X** in the appropriate blank. (If students do not have copies of the sample paper, they can write on separate sheets of paper.)
4. Ask students to compare their responses with those of a partner. They should take a few minutes to talk about the paper and ask each other questions.
5. After three or four minutes, ask students to share their reasons for scoring the paper as they did.

Discussing the Paper

Discuss the paper with the class. Ask students to say what scores they gave the paper and why. The *why* is the most important part in deepening their understanding. Use the following questions to encourage discussion:

- Did you find many errors in this writing? A few errors? No errors at all?
- How much editing would need to be done to prepare this paper for publication?
- How do conventions affect voice and ideas in this paper?

*Rationale for the Score**

Most students should see this paper as **strong.** It received a **6,** based on the 6-point rubric. Although it has some minor errors, it is very clean copy and would be ready to publish with just two touchups: Add an apostrophe to *it's* in the third sentence of the first paragraph, and insert a comma following *though* in the third sentence of the third paragraph.

Extensions

1. Ask each student to review a piece of his or her own writing and to mark any errors using editor's symbols. Then, have them trade papers with partners for review and discussion. If any disagreement occurs, refer to the *Write Source 2000* handbook. (See Teacher's Guide page 96.)
2. Invite students to ask you several "I've always wondered about that" types of questions involving conventions. Model answers on the overhead. If you need help answering a question, refer to the *Write Source 2000* handbook to show students how easy it is to find the answers to questions about conventions.

*See Teacher's Guide page 198 for a 5-point rubric and page 213 for the score based on that rubric.

name: .... date: ....

Sample Paper 23: CONVENTIONS

Golf Mania

My father is totally hooked on golf (no pun intended). The odd thing is that he does not play very well. In fact, he rarely hits par; and when he does, its a surprise even to him. He just loves "getting out there," as he calls it.

Weather does not worry him. Like many avid golfers, Dad will play rain or shine. About the only things that bring him in are thunderstorms and blizzards. Under those conditions, the course is usually closed anyway. I have seen him play in wind so strong it whipped the hat right off his head. He didn't even look up. He was focusing on his shot.

Dad can tee off pretty well. He hardly ever hits the middle of the fairway, but he can drive the ball pretty far. When it comes to putting, though it's another story completely. Dad might get on the green (the final playing area) in just two strokes, but then it takes him six more to get the ball in the hole. You might expect him to get very frustrated by this, but he is having such a good time that he doesn't seem to notice.

Mark the score that this paper should receive in the trait of CONVENTIONS. Read your rubric for Conventions to help you decide. Then write your reason for the score.

____ 1 ____ 2 ____ 3 ____ 4 ____ 5 ____ 6

____

____

Sample Paper 24: Why Do I Need a Job?

Objectives

Students will enhance their skills by identifying conventional errors through silent and oral reading.

Materials

Student Rubric for Conventions (Teacher's Guide page 95)
Sample Paper 24: Why Do I Need a Job? (Teacher's Guide page 191 and/or Overhead 24)

Scoring the Paper

1. Distribute copies of the sample paper and the Student Rubric for Conventions. Use the rubric to focus students' attention on the key features of the trait of CONVENTIONS. Students should look for missing or repeated words and any errors in spelling, punctuation, grammar, and capitalization.
2. Have students think about these questions as they read the paper: *Does the writer make just one or two kinds of errors—or many kinds of errors? Does the writer use conventions skillfully to make this paper easy to follow?*
3. Ask students to score the paper individually, using the student rubric. They should mark their scores in writing, putting an **X** in the appropriate blank. (If students do not have copies of the sample paper, they can write on separate sheets of paper.)
4. Ask students to compare their responses with those of a partner. They should take a few minutes to talk about the paper and ask each other questions.
5. After three or four minutes, ask students to share their reasons for scoring the paper as they did.

Discussing the Paper

Discuss the paper with the class. Ask students to say what scores they gave the paper and why. The *why* is the most important part in deepening their understanding. Use the following questions to encourage discussion:

- Do you find many errors in this writing? A few errors? No errors at all?
- Do errors in punctuation make dialogue difficult to follow?
- How much editing would need to be done to prepare this paper for publication?

*Rationale for the Score**

Most students should see this paper as **in process.** It received a **3,** based on the 6-point rubric. Although many things are done correctly, repeated errors in punctuating dialogue make this writing somewhat confusing. Though most readers will get through the text without undue difficulty, there are sufficient errors (31) to slow down a reader.

Extensions

1. Ask each student to review a piece of his or her own writing and to use editor's symbols to mark any errors. Students should use these strategies to find errors: read the piece more than once; read it aloud at least one time; read it at least once from the bottom of the page up (yes!) in order to find double words, spelling errors, or other mistakes that may be hard to spot in normal reading.
2. Have students create editing lessons that feature dialogue. Ask them to use word processing programs, if possible, to design a dialogue between two speakers. Lessons should run up to eight lines, have several errors in conventions, and be double-spaced. Student partners can exchange lessons and respond to each other's work.
3. As a class, brainstorm a list of the Top Ten Most Easily Overlooked Editing Errors. Keep the list posted for everyone to see. (This can also be a small-group activity if you would like to generate multiple posters.)

*See Teacher's Guide page 198 for a 5-point rubric and page 213 for the score based on that rubric.

name: .... date: ....

Sample Paper 24: CONVENTIONS

Why Do I Need a Job?

"You should think about getting a job this Summer, my mom told me. This was right after she told me to clean my room. "Why do i need a job?" I asked? "For college, of course. she answered."

Good grief! I'm only in eighth grade, I said. I have lots of time to save money for college. "Not really," was her anser. "It gets here fast than you think. She says that about everything

I'm too young for a job, I told her. no one will hire me. I'm only 13. You can mow lawns, pull weeds, babysit, run errands, or do a million other things" my mom told me. She always thinks other people need to work harder! "I dont think I can make enough money babysitting put myself through college, I said.

Don't whine! was her response. I figured it out. I will need to babysit for something like 10,000 hours to pay for first year in college. "I better get get started."

Mark the score that this paper should receive in the trait of CONVENTIONS. Read your rubric for Conventions to help you decide. Then write your reason for the score.

___ 1 ___ 2 ___ 3 ___ 4 ___ 5 ___ 6

____

____

Appendix

Using a 5-Point Rubric

For your convenience, we have included in this appendix 5-point student and teacher rubrics for each trait, as well as scores for each Sample Paper based on the 5-point rubric. Although we have always recommended the 6-point rubric, the 5-point rubric has certain advantages.

The 5-point rubric is simple to use and to internalize. Performance is defined at only three levels: **weak** (point 1), **in process** (point 3), and **strong,** or proficient (point 5). The 4 and the 2 on the 5-point scale are compromise scores. Therefore, if a performance is slightly stronger than a 3 but not quite strong enough to warrant a 5, it would receive a 4. Because raters think in terms of "weak," "in process," and "strong" in assigning scores, this is a simple system to follow.

Few differences exist conceptually between these rubrics. Remember that the key reason to use rubrics with students is to teach the concepts: *ideas, organization, voice, word choice, sentence fluency,* and *conventions.* We want students to understand what we mean, for example, by good *organization,* and one way of doing this is to have them score writing samples. The particular rubric used is less important than whether a student sees a paper as weak, strong, or somewhere between those two points. We want students to distinguish between writing that works and writing that needs revision. Whether they define a strong performance as a 5 or 6 is much less important than whether they understand why a paper is strong or weak. The numbers are merely a kind of shorthand that allows students and teachers to discuss competency in simple terms.

We hope that these distinctions help clarify the very slight differences between these rubrics. Use the rubric with which you are most familiar or with which you feel most comfortable.

Student Rubric for

Ideas

5 My paper is clear, focused, detailed, and engaging.

- My main idea is crystal clear throughout the paper. This writing is engaging and informative.
- The reader can tell that I know a lot about this topic.
- I chose details that are important and interesting and hold the reader's attention.
- I left out the "filler." Details relate clearly to my main idea or story.
- My topic is narrowly focused and manageable.

3 My paper is clear enough to follow and fairly focused, but I need to include more information. Some of my details are too general.

- I think the reader can tell what my main idea is.
- I know some things about this topic. If I knew more, I could make this really interesting and informative.
- Some of my "details" are things most people already know.
- Some information is not really needed. It's just filler.
- This topic sure feels wide—maybe I'm trying to tell too much.

1 I'm still working on what I want to say.

- I don't know what my main idea is. I'm still working on it.
- Help! I don't know enough about this topic to write.
- I need better details. I'm just making things up as I go.
- I'm mostly writing to fill space. I'm hoping a good topic will come to me as I write.
- I don't know whether my topic is too wide or too narrow—I'm not sure what my topic is!

Student Rubric for

Organization

5 My paper is logical and easy to follow—it's as if I'm holding a flashlight for readers.

- My lead grabs the reader's attention and makes him or her want to read on.
- Every detail seems to be in the right order.
- My paper follows a pattern that works really well for this topic.
- I built strong bridges between sentences by using transitional words.
- My conclusion brings things to closure and leaves the reader thinking.

3 The reader can follow this, I think. The light is fading—but it's there!

- My lead might need to be livelier—but at least it's there.
- Most details are in the proper order.
- I think I followed a pattern. I need to check.
- I used some transitions. They might not be strong ones though.
- My conclusion is OK. It might not make the reader think too hard, but it's there.

1 This paper is hard to follow—like walking in the dark without a flashlight!

- I don't really have a lead. I just started writing.
- I wrote things down as they came into my head. I am not sure the order works.
- I don't see any real pattern here.
- I wasn't sure how to connect ideas, so I didn't worry about transitions.
- I don't really have a conclusion. My paper just ends.

Student Rubric for

Voice

5 My voice is strong and individual. The reader can tell it's my voice!

- The reader will want to share this paper aloud.
- I love this topic, and my enthusiasm will get the reader hooked, too.
- I'm writing for a particular audience, and I've considered the interests and needs of this audience.
- I've used just the right voice for this topic. It fits like a glove.

3 You can hear me in the writing *sometimes.* My voice comes and goes.

- The reader may want to share some parts of this paper aloud.
- I couldn't get excited about this topic; the reader can hear that in my writing.
- I thought about my audience sometimes, but not always!
- I think the voice I've used is OK for this topic.

1 I don't hear that much voice in this writing.

- The reader probably won't want to share this paper aloud.
- This topic seemed totally boring to me. I guess I sound bored, too.
- I just wanted this to be over with. I do not care if anyone reads it.
- I don't think my voice fits this topic very well. It should be stronger, or different.

Student Rubric for

Word Choice

5 Every single word I chose helps make my message clear, memorable, and interesting.

- Strong verbs consistently give my writing energy.
- I cut the clutter. I made every word count.
- I used sensory language to help the reader see, hear, feel, taste, or smell.
- If I used new or unusual words, I tried to make the meaning clear from context.

3 Most words and phrases are clear. A few words may be too general—or misused.

- Some of my verbs have power. Some could use more muscle.
- I got rid of some clutter, but this still has its wordy moments.
- I missed some opportunities to use sensory language.
- I did use some new or unusual words—but I'm not sure I made their meanings clear.

1 My words are hard to understand. I am not always sure about what I'm trying to say.

- My verbs are ordinary.
- Some parts of my writing are wordy; in other parts, I didn't say enough.
- I did not worry about sounds, smells, tastes, and feelings. I just used the first words I thought of.
- I didn't even know the meanings of all these words, so it was hard to make them clear for the reader.

Student Rubric for

Sentence Fluency

5 My writing is smooth, natural sounding, and easy to read aloud.

- The reader can easily read this aloud with the kind of expression that brings out voice and meaning.
- The reader will see plenty of variety in sentence length and structure.
- I avoided run-on sentences and repetitive or choppy writing.
- My dialogue (if I used any) sounds like real people talking.

3 Most of my writing is smooth. I might have some choppy sentences or run-ons.

- The reader won't stumble reading this aloud. But it might be hard to get in enough expression to bring out the voice or meaning.
- A lot of my sentences begin the same way. Many are the same length, too.
- Although I revised, I may have missed some run-ons or other sentence problems.
- If I used dialogue, it needs work. Sometimes the people sound real, and sometimes they don't.

1 This is hard to read, even for me! I can't tell one sentence from another.

- I think the reader would have to work hard to read this aloud.
- It's hard to tell where my sentences begin and end. I'm not sure how long they are—or whether they begin in different ways.
- I am quite sure that I have run-on sentences or other sentence problems. This needs a lot of revision before it reads smoothly.
- If I used dialogue, I do not think it is effective. It needs work.

Student Rubric for

Conventions

5 The reader will have a hard time finding errors in this paper. It's ready to publish.

- I used conventions correctly to make the meaning clear.
- I checked spelling, punctuation, grammar and usage, and capitalization. They are all correct.
- I read the paper silently and aloud. I corrected every mistake I saw or heard.

3 The reader will probably notice some errors. I need to read this once more—and really be careful this time!

- I did a lot of things just right, but I also made mistakes. Some errors might slow the reader down or make my message unclear.
- Although I checked my spelling, punctuation, grammar, and capitalization, I think there are too many errors.
- I read my paper quickly but should read it again. Maybe if I read it aloud, my ears would catch mistakes my eyes missed.

1 I made so many mistakes that I have a hard time reading this myself.

- This paper is so full of errors that it's hard to spot the things I did right.
- I forgot to check a lot of my spelling, punctuation, grammar, and capitalization.
- I did not read this—silently or aloud. I guess I should have.

Teacher Rubric for

Ideas

5 The paper has a clear, well-focused main idea and interesting, carefully chosen details that go beyond the obvious to support or expand that main idea.

- The main idea is easy to identify and understand. It's also well defined and small enough to be manageable.
- The writer seems to know the topic well and uses his or her knowledge to advantage.
- Details enhance the main idea and enlighten the reader.
- Unnecessary information has been omitted.

3 The paper is clear for the most part, but the reader needs more information. Development is skeletal, or the topic may be so broad that it is hard to cover in the scope of the paper.

- The main idea is clear or can be inferred.
- The writer seems to have a general grasp of the topic.
- Generalities abound, but a few little-known, significant, or intriguing details are also present.
- Some information is unnecessary.

1 The writer is searching for a topic or a way to narrow a topic that is too broad to handle effectively.

- The main idea is unclear. It is hard to figure out what the writer is trying to say.
- The writer displays limited knowledge of the topic—or it may be hard to tell what the main idea is. Or, the topic may be so broad that there is just no way to bring it into focus.
- Details seem general and random. They do not support or expand any larger message.
- Much of the writing simply fills space, as if the writer is struggling to find things to say.

Teacher Rubric for

Organization

5 This paper is logical and easy to follow.

- The lead grabs the reader's attention and sets up what follows.
- Every detail seems to come at the right time and in the right place.
- The paper follows an identifiable pattern that is well suited to the topic.
- It is easy for the reader to make connections, thanks to the writer's skillful use of transitions.
- The conclusion brings closure without being too abrupt or too drawn out.

3 The reader can follow the direction of the paper most of the time.

- The paper has a lead. It does not grab the reader's attention though.
- Most details come in the right order and at the right time.
- A pattern may not be immediately recognizable, but it works.
- The writer uses some transitions; some are missing or weak. Some ideas feel "tacked on" or irrelevant.
- The paper has a conclusion. It may or may not offer a strong sense of resolution.

1 This paper is hard to follow.

- There is no real lead. The writer just begins the paper.
- It is very difficult to connect details or thoughts to one another or to any main idea.
- It is difficult to identify any pattern within the writing.
- Transitions are weak or missing altogether.
- The paper just ends. There is no sense of closure or resolution.

Teacher Rubric for

Voice

5 The writing is highly individual. It bears the definite imprint of this writer.

- The reader will want to share this paper aloud.
- The writer seems engaged by the topic, and strong personal energy and commitment are evident in every line.
- The writer is clearly writing to a particular audience.
- The voice is totally appropriate for the topic and purpose.

3 The reader can hear the writer's voice now and again. The voice comes and goes.

- The reader might share moments aloud, even if the reader does not share the whole paper.
- The writer seems reasonably at home with the topic but less than enthusiastic. Bursts of energy mix with lulls.
- This writer *could* be writing for a particular audience—or just to get the job done.
- The voice is acceptable for the topic and audience.

1 It would be difficult to identify this writer. The voice is not powerful or strongly individual.

- This paper is not yet ready to be shared aloud.
- The writer sounds a little bored or tired; perhaps this topic did not work for him or her. It is hard to sense *any* personal engagement.
- The writer does not seem to be reaching out to any particular audience.
- The voice is not suited to the topic. It needs to be stronger—or just different in tone.

Teacher Rubric for

Word Choice

5 Every word makes the writing clear and interesting.

- Strong verbs energize the writing.
- This writing is concise. Every word counts.
- Sensory words (as appropriate) help readers see, hear, feel, taste, or smell what is happening.
- The writer makes meaning clear from context.

3 Most words and phrases are clear; some may be vague or misused. Fine writing is weakened by fuzzy or overdone language.

- A *few* strong verbs give life to the writing—more would help.
- Clutter makes the text wordy, or the writing is too sketchy to convey the message.
- The writer uses some sensory language—but also misses opportunities.
- Meaning is sometimes clear from context, sometimes not.

1 Many words are hard to understand. Language has too much jargon, is too general, or is misused.

- The writer does not rely on verbs. As a result, the language is flat, or modifiers may be overdone.
- The writing is so insufficient that it is hard to make sense of it. Or, it is so wordy that the reader becomes overwhelmed.
- The writer does not make effective use of sensory language to help bring the topic or story to life.
- The writer does not use context to make word meanings clear. In fact, it is often difficult to determine what the writer is trying to say.

Teacher Rubric for

Sentence Fluency

5 The writing is smooth, natural, and easy to read aloud.

- The reader can read this with expression—like a good film script.
- Almost all the sentences begin in different ways. Some are long, some short. Variety abounds.
- The writer avoids choppy writing, ineffective repetition, or run-ons.
- If dialogue is used, it sounds like real conversation.

3 This writing features well-crafted sentences interspersed with choppy moments or run-ons.

- Although this text is fairly easy to read aloud, it may not invite the kind of expression needed to bring out the meaning or voice.
- Too many sentences begin the same way. Too many sentences are about the same length.
- Some choppy sentences, run-ons, or repetition could slow a reader down.
- Dialogue, if used, does not reflect real conversation.

1 This writing is difficult to read aloud.

- The reader will need to rehearse to read this aloud—and will need to do some on-the-spot editing.
- It's sometimes hard to tell where sentences begin and end. Variety in sentence lengths or beginnings is minimal.
- Choppy writing, repetition, run-ons or other sentence problems abound.
- The writer has not attempted dialogue. If dialogue is used, it does not sound like real conversation.

Teacher Rubric for

Conventions

5 The writer is in control of conventions, and this paper is essentially ready to publish.

- The writer has used conventions correctly to help make the meaning clear.
- The spelling, punctuation, grammar, and capitalization are all, for the most part, correct.
- The writer has read the paper both silently and aloud and has corrected errors. It looks and sounds polished.

3 A good, careful proofreading and editing will prepare this text for publication.

- A few noticeable errors may slow the reader somewhat, but they do not seriously affect meaning.
- Spelling, punctuation, grammar, and capitalization are working at a functional level. Careful editing would help.
- The writer has read the paper at least once, but a second reading—silent or oral—could help reveal additional errors.

1 This writer is not yet in control of conventions. Many errors need to be corrected before this text is ready to publish.

- Many errors slow the reader down and get in the way of the writer's message.
- There are many errors in spelling, punctuation, grammar, and capitalization.
- The writer has not read this paper silently or aloud. It needs significant attention from the writer and (perhaps) an editing partner.

Rationales for the Scores Using the 5-point Rubric

Unit 1: Ideas

Sample Paper 1: *If I Were Stranded*

Rationale for the Score

Most students should see this paper as **strong.** It received a score of **5,** based on the 5-point rubric. This writing has a clear main idea, and the writer never loses focus on that main idea. The writer gives reasons for his or her choice and also explores (briefly) the folly of other possible choices. Without putting in too many details, the writer explains that fishing could be entertaining and that it could relieve loneliness and boredom while sharpening other skills. The ironic twist at the end is a nice touch.

Sample Paper 2: *Energy—A Problem!*

Rationale for the Score

Most students should see this paper as **in process.** It received a score of **3,** based on the 5-point rubric. It is quite simple to infer this writer's main idea: we should all be concerned about energy problems. However, the writing is not focused. It deals with issues of pollution, energy sources that should or could be explored, and ways to conserve energy. The writer also introduces the topic of education early on but does not follow up. The paper tries to cover too much territory; as a result, it covers nothing in depth. The writer needs to know the topic better in order to share new, important, and interesting information.

Sample Paper 3: *The Most Beautiful Thing*

Rationale for the Score

Most students should see this paper as **in process.** It received a score of **3,** based on the 5-point rubric. Although the main idea (moths are beautiful creatures) is easy to infer, the writer does not paint a clear picture. Readers know that moths have colorful markings and patterns. But readers need precise, vivid descriptions. What colors? What patterns? In addition, the writer goes off-track at the end with comments about the destruction of crops and the short life of moths. This information has nothing to do with the moths' appearance. It might be possible to tie these comments to the main idea, but the writer does not do so.

Sample Paper 4: *Sea Horses*

Rationale for the Score

Most students should see this paper as **strong.** It received a **5,** based on the 5-point rubric. It is highly focused and has a strong main idea: the sea horse is a fragile, unusual creature that needs protection to survive. Everything in the paper relates to this idea (which is never directly stated). This paper is a good example of what sound informational writing should be. It informs the reader by presenting a rich array of details. Though this writer shares many facts, they are not piled on in encyclopedic fashion; for example, the image of the sea horse sucking up food like a tiny vacuum cleaner paints a vivid and lively picture. This paper would likely score high in voice as well.

Unit 2: Organization

Sample Paper 5: *My Idea of Art*

Rationale for the Score

Most students should see this paper as **in process.** It received a score of **2,** based on the 5-point rubric, because the observations are randomly made rather than closely connected. The lead is indefinite: what is meant by "weird stuff"? The conclusion is a platitude: art is important to the world. The paper does not support this conclusion. With the exception of architecture, the writer does not seem to care much about art. The writer first needs to define his or her topic and then stick with it, connecting all details to the main idea as well as to each other.

Sample Paper 6: *Camping? No Thanks!*

Rationale for the Score

Most students should see this paper as **strong.** It received a score of **5,** based on the 5-point rubric, because it has a very strong lead and conclusion and is easy to follow. The writer follows a definite time-order pattern, wrapping up with conclusions about how he or she feels. The transitions are especially strong: *Camping starts . . . This is the part . . . Later, when we're around the campfire . . .* The writer uses the notation "Part II: On the Trail" to introduce one segment of the paper, but this strategy is inconsistent throughout the paper. However, the designation does not disrupt the flow of ideas.

Sample Paper 7: *Monster*

Rationale for the Score

Most students should see this paper as **in process.** It received a score of **3,** based on the 5-point rubric, because the lead is weak, the conclusion just stops, and the order is poor. Transitions are weak, but this is not surprising because the paper leaps from point to point without connecting ideas. In addition, the writer offers unnecessary details (wandering around the park, getting scared when skiing). The paper could be condensed.

Sample Paper 8: *Insects—Learn to Love Them!*

Rationale for the Score

Most students should see this paper as **strong.** It received a score of **4,** based on the 5-point rubric, because it begins and ends effectively. Transitions are strong, too, though the connection between the second and third paragraph could be improved. The writer moves abruptly from stating that humans are not able to live without insects to claiming that humans believe that they control the earth; the two ideas are related, but the writer does not make the link clear. The paper is well focused, however, and centers consistently on this main idea: insects, though pesky, help keep us alive.

Unit 3: Voice

Sample Paper 9: *Maps*

Rationale for the Score

Most students should see this paper as **in process.** It received a score of **2,** based on the 5-point rubric. Although it has moments of strong voice, the voice is not consistently strong throughout the paper. The writer explains his or her frustration, but we do not feel the frustration. In fact, the writer sometimes sounds downright bored with the topic: *This is fun . . . Sometimes it was hard . . . Sometimes we had to stop to ask for directions . . .* These listless comments make readers feel as sleepy as if they were on a long road trip, too. The writer should become more engaged with this topic or select another topic.

Sample Paper 10: *A Gift for Giving*

Rationale for the Score

Most students should see this paper as **fairly strong.** It received a score of **4,** based on the 5-point rubric, because it is sincere and seems to be an honest tribute to a grandmother the writer obviously loves. Some parts, such as the description of the swearing on the freeway, are stronger than others. The voice fades a bit, for instance, in the conclusion. What is missing, though, is the grandmother herself. Readers cannot hear her voice. Also, although the examples are wonderful, none of them are developed. For instance, readers cannot see Shirley and the narrator reading from the mystery novel or hear them speaking. We don't get Shirley's reaction when her dog has puppies. With some dialogue and expansion of one or two examples, this paper would score better.

Sample Paper 11: *Miss Obnoxious*

Rationale for the Score

Most students should see this paper as **strong.** It received a **5,** based on the 5-point rubric. It has humor, energy, individuality, and is fun to read, whether silently or aloud. In many places, good use of detail helps make the voice strong. The closing is understated and maintains the humor. This writer paints a vivid portrait of himself as a victim. Notice the use of dialogue, which also contributes to voice.

Sample Paper 12: *Tornado*

Rationale for the Score

Most students should see this paper as **in process.** It received a score of **2,** based on the 5-point rubric. The voice is not strong. (The writer sounds more like the calm before the storm rather than the storm itself!) The writer makes casual observations about the events that occurred but conveys no sense of urgency or panic—or even much concern, for that matter. This account has little energy—readers must wonder whether the writer truly was frightened by this experience.

Unit 4: Word Choice

Sample Paper 13: *Mature Audiences Only*

Rationale for the Score

Most students should see this paper as **strong.** It received a score of **5,** based on the 5-point rubric. Though "Mature Audiences Only" will not send readers scrambling for the dictionary, it does contain some fresh, original use of everyday language: *we'd develop a preference for thought-provoking entertainment.* In addition, the piece is peppered generously with strong verbs: *wonder, express,* and *squeezing.* Strong word choice clarifies meaning and enhances voice, which in this paper seems self-assured and informed. The writing is not wordy and repetitive, nor is it overwritten.

Sample Paper 14: *Having Braces*

Rationale for the Score

Most students should see this paper as **in process.** It received a **2,** based on the 5-point rubric. Though the basic meaning is reasonably clear, the paper needs stronger verbs and more vivid, precise language. Many words are repeated, making the writing cluttered and imprecise. Nearly every reader knows something about the experience of getting braces. Readers need more precise and interesting word choices that provide a new perspective or personal impression.

Sample Paper 15: *Planting Tomatoes*

Rationale for the Score

Most students should see this paper as **in process.** It received a **2,** based on the 5-point rubric, because the piece is filled with overwritten phrases that simply do not work. These may have come from the writer's imagination, but they seem to be evidence of thesaurus overuse: *the enterprise of planting tomatoes with euphoria and zest, the most prestigious tomatoes, a vivacious tomato plant, implant the tomato,* and so on. The result is a hard-to-read piece on a simple topic: How to plant a tomato. This lofty language is overkill with such a simple subject, which is why readers might be distracted from the message.

Sample Paper 16: *Go with the Flow!*

Rationale for the Score

Most students should see this paper as **fairly strong.** It received a **4,** based on the 5-point rubric. The language is clear and refreshing, like the river ride itself, and contains some strong moments: *smooth and tranquil; foamy water; we were drenched; slippery, silky waters; spinning like a giant Frisbee;* and *conquered our fear.* Some of the language is a bit predictable: *our aching arms* and *we were all smiles.* These expressions are clear and help provide a picture of the raft going down the rapids. Yet the writer might have stretched a bit harder to provide original phrasing and details for someone who hasn't experienced river rafting. On the other hand, the words are never confusing or overwritten.

Unit 5: Sentence Fluency

Sample Paper 17: *Mosquitoes, Beware!*

Rationale for the Score

Most students should see this paper as still **in process.** It received a **3,** based on the 5-point rubric (some students may see it as a 2), because it is extremely choppy and so difficult to read with inflection. The sentences are nearly all the same length. Further, many sentences begin with the words *this, if,* or *it.* Though the word *mosquitoes* is not often used as a sentence starter, it is repeated so many times that the repetition disrupts the fluency. In addition, sentence beginnings provide virtually no link between ideas; the writer does not make use of transitional phrases, such as *in the meantime* and *on the other hand.* On the positive side, the writer uses complete sentences and has included no run-ons.

Sample Paper 18: *Hold the Garlic, Please!*

Rationale for the Score

Most students should see this paper as **strong.** We gave it a **5,** based on the 5-point rubric. The sentences vary in both length and structure. The shortest is only three words long and the longest contains twenty-nine words. Students should not become too formulaic or statistical in their analysis of writing, but this count verifies the extent of variety in this piece. Virtually every sentence begins in a slightly different way (compare Sample Paper 17). Reading the paper aloud expressively helps bring out voice.

Sample Paper 19: *It's for You*

Rationale for the Score

Most students should see this paper as **strong.** It received a **4,** based on the 5-point rubric, because it is varied in structure and sentence length and is easy to read. In addition, the dialogue is natural and works well. It only misses receiving a score of 5 because many sentences begin with *we, he,* or *I*—and it does not have the variety in sentence length of Sample Paper 18 ("Hold the Garlic, Please!").

Sample Paper 20: *Moving*

Rationale for the Score

Most students should see this paper as **in process.** It received a **2,** based on the 5-point rubric, because it is quite difficult to read aloud. Some sentences are run-ons and clearly need to be separated. Others, though, are joined by connecting words, such as *and,* and are much too long. Extra words should be crossed out, extra connectives eliminated, and run-ons repaired.

Unit 6: Conventions

Sample Paper 21: *Handling Food Carefully*

Rationale for the Score

Most students should see this paper as **in process.** It received a **2,** based on the 5-point rubric. Although it is possible to decipher the writer's message, the many errors in conventions slow a reader down. Further, there are many types of errors, including missing words, extra words, misspellings, omitted commas, extra commas, omitted capital letters, an omitted period, and omitted apostrophes. This text would need extensive editing to be ready for publication.

Sample Paper 22: *Worms—They're Everywhere*

Rationale for the Score

Most students should see this paper as **fairly strong.** It received a **3,** based on the 5-point rubric. Although the paper does not have many errors, there are enough that a careful reader will notice them. On the other hand, errors do not seriously interfere with readability. This might be termed a "lightly edited" piece; another careful editing will prepare it for publication.

Sample Paper 23: *Golf Mania*

Rationale for the Score

Most students should see this paper as **strong.** It received a **5,** based on the 5-point rubric. Although it has some minor errors, it is very clean copy and would be ready to publish with just two touchups: Add an apostrophe to *it's* in the third sentence of the first paragraph, and insert a comma following *though* in the third sentence of the third paragraph.

Sample Paper 24: *Why Do I Need a Job?*

Rationale for the Score

Most students should see this paper as **in process.** It received a **2,** based on the 5-point rubric. Although many things are done correctly, repeated errors in punctuating dialogue make this writing somewhat confusing. Though most readers will get through the text without undue difficulty, there are sufficient errors (31) to slow down a reader.